No More Secondhand Art

No More Secondhand Art

AWAKENING THE ARTIST WITHIN

Peter London

SHAMBHALA

Boston & London

1989

Shambhala Publications, Inc.
Horticultural Hall
300 Massachusetts Avenue
Boston, Massachusetts 02115

Photographs by Peter London, Katherine Rubenstein, and
Katherine Walz

9   8   7   6   5

Printed in the United States of America on acid-free paper   ∞

Distributed in the United States by Random House, Inc., and
in Canada by Random House of Canada Ltd

Library of Congress Cataloging-in-Publication Data

London, Peter.
    No more secondhand art: awakening the artist within /
Peter London
        p.   cm.
    ISBN 0-87773-482-8
    1. Art—Psychology. 2. Creativity in art. 1. Title.
N7LL597   1989   89-42618
701'.15—dc20   CIP

To Harry London

What if imagination and art are not frosting at all, but the fountainhead of human experience?

—*Rollo May*

Contents

Preface

Making images is as natural a human endeavor as speaking. The necessity to communicate with the world underlies both, and both are means to touch, explore, and create the world. Both verbal and visual language develop very early in life and are soon practiced by all children. Just as verbal language is described by Noam Chomsky as a generic function of the human brain, Rudolf Arnheim, the psychologist of visual perception, ascribes the same origins of visual thinking to the organic functions of the brain. However, whereas all normally functioning people, having once learned to speak, go on speaking throughout their life, very few people continue making images. Most of us are severed from this native ability to visually "speak." It would seem that a major contributing factor must be how we have been taught to make images. We have *learned* to be embarrassed by our efforts. We have *learned* to feel so inept and disenfranchised from our own visual expressions that we simply cease doing it altogether. Only our dreaming mind continues to make images throughout our life, and even these we erase upon awakening.

There are some disabling myths about what art is, how to do it, what is good art, and what art is for, that have gagged generations, depriving them of a significant and natural means of expression. This is a terrible loss and an unnecessary one. The purpose of this book is to address that situation and return visual expression as a natural and full language to every person and to enable everyone to employ this means of expression to do what all language does, to speak about the world as it is, and to create a world of our choosing.

This book means to help you uncover your natural image-making abilities and so to return to you the power that language has to share and create life. We must recapture our personal and idiosyncratic language so that we may speak about our personal and idiosyncratic *life*. The claim is not that our triumphs in art will automatically lead to similar successes in life. The claim put forward is more modest but nonetheless substantial; it is that the ways of thinking about what art is, what art has the potential of doing, and the strategies offered herein, are powerful means of awakening the artist within.

The potential of carry over from art to the transformation of a life is real—not simple or automatic, but real. It is this personal transformation of life through an engagement with the creative process that this book seeks.

The origins of the thinking that is presented here began in conversations with my teachers, students, and colleagues; the most important of these occurred between myself and a long-time friend and fellow artist, Seymour Segal. Together we designed and taught a course entitled Drawing from Within. Five years of collaboration in teaching the course and many, many hours of conversation about how art and life reflect and inform each other shape the major perceptions of this book. The course was designed around a series of Creative Encounters. More than and different from "art lessons," these Encounters sought to challenge the student in such a fashion as to require introspection for their full and necessary creative response. In the process of drawing from within for the sources of their visual expression, participants began to uncover their artistic self, dormant and neglected as it may have been. The awakening of this artistic and visually minded self brought about an invigorated imagery, deeper at the root and higher in ambition.

Just as the ideas presented here were generated in dialogue, the book is written in conversational style, as if you and I are sitting in my studio talking together. You show me some of your work, I show you some of mine, and we talk about where we got stuck, where we triumphed, and better ways of thinking about the issues, problems, and glories of the creative enterprise. Having taught thousands of people over twenty-five years, certain basic and important questions and issues seem always to arise in their conversation: What is art? (Not the thing but the process.) Where do you begin? How do I know if it's good? If art is more than decoration, what else is it? How can I use art not only to speak about the world I know and feel, but also to explore the world, explore myself, define myself, expand myself? My experience as an artist, a teacher, and an art therapist convinces me that not the lack of technical skills but the inadequate and wrong-headed responses to these questions are what silence us and keep the artist within dormant. In the course of the book, ways of rethinking these issues will be offered which have proven to be enabling for others. I am hopeful that they will be so for you.

The opening section of the book declares a new agenda for the encounter with art. The purpose of making art is seen first as the creation of a preferred self rather than an inherited self; subsequently as the creation of things, which celebrates and enhances the world. This section is composed of brief essays that explore this general theme and sets the domain of art, expanded upon in subsequent sections. The overarching conception of art and its purposes posited herein is that what we are and what we were is not yet all that we might become and that the creative process is a powerful vehicle to probe what may lie ahead.

Chapter 2 describes the many elements underlying creative endeavors of which most people are unaware. The inattention to these creative predispositions dooms subsequent attempts at creative expression to disappointment and frustration. An examination of these critical elements allowing for natural, powerful, expressive images to come forth is the subject of this chapter.

Creative Encounters differ substantially from the usual art lessons or art projects encountered in art schools. These Encounters are initiated by first having an authentic encounter with a significant event, question, or issue, one that demands a full, reflective response. The ultimate issue, always at the center of each such experience, is the question "Who am I?" Each experience investigates and celebrates a different dimension of this infinite, fascinating, and empowering question. Design principles for formulating Creative Encounters are the subject of chapter 3.

Having taught the Drawing from Within workshops for the last five years in a number of settings with a variety of students of all ages and abilities, I have found a number of Creative Encounters to stand out as particularly rewarding. A dozen such experiences are offered in chapter 4 to illustrate what the philosophy and principles of the text may look like in actual practice.

Chapter 5 deals with the materials and strategies of art making. Art supplies connotes things found in art stores and supply closets: canvas, brushes, and paint. *Media* is a more inclusive term, and in its meaning lie vaster, more powerful domains for creative expression. Media are those things which stand between imagination and expression, between the mind and the act. Media are transformative devices, leveraging the mind, the hand, and the will.

Employing the creative process as a means of personal and artistic transformation is a rigorous experience that, when successful, brings about substantial changes not only in the look of one's art, but in the quality of one's life. Integrating this "evolved self" with familiar companions and settings requires deliberate care. This final section of the book serves as a coda to the whole and suggests ways of returning to old friends in new ways.

The antecedents for the thesis presented in this book are many and diffuse. The earliest have to do with those incidents that helped me to define myself as an artist. In kindergarten, I remember drawing a picture of a steam locomotive puffing along the tracks. The engine was gray, the tracks were black, and I thought light green grass would look good growing through the tracks. When I showed the drawing to my teacher, Miss Goldberg, she said, "Rocks are under the tracks, not grass, but your grass looks better. Very nice."

In the fourth grade my friend Frankie came over to play. He liked one of my drawings that I had pinned to my wall—so much so that he stole it. I think that was nice too, although I didn't think so then.

My dad got up every Saturday morning at 7:00 A.M. to drive me an hour to Pratt's children's art classes, then waited around for two hours to take me home again. He did that for about five years.

In high school I called my art teacher, Mr. Frankel, at home about some of my paintings. He said, Come over to my house and let's take a look. We sat in his garden for a couple of hours, just the two of us talking about my work.

My wife said, "I love you most when you smell from oil paints and linseed oil." I never, ever use acrylics.

Many such acts of care shape a life and firm a fledgling identity as an artist. These and a thousand others confirmed me. As these encounters served me, I hope your encounter with the ideas in this book serve to awaken the artist within you.

Acknowledgments

I came to hold the views I have concerning the transformative powers of art as a consequence of myriad encounters directly with or through the works of especially gifted people. Embedded as these encounters are throughout my lifetime, how to acknowledge them all and how ever to be sufficient in words of gratitude? Saying precisely and concisely who these people are and what their contributions were exceeds my talents. This preamble is needed to suggest the magnitude of my indebtedness and the inadequacy of my means to explain why. With this caveat in mind, I say to the following

John Dewey, Käthe Kollwitz, Martin Buber, Philip Frankel, Hermann Hesse, Tom Thomson, Dwayne Heubner, W. Eugene Smith, Cynthia Ozick, my students, Henri Matisse, Joseph Campbell, Alfie Pinsky, Philip Roth, Annie Dillard, Seymour Segal, Marion, Jonathan, Danielle, Jean, Harry, Jane, Ross, D. T. Suzuki, Howard Evans, Paolo Knell, Dorothea Lange, Jacob Bronowski, Otto Rank, Teilhard de Chardin, Marv Hiles, Jean Paul Sartre, Johannes Brahms, Pablo Neruda, Charlie Beck, Buckminster Fuller, James Kaput, John Cage, Al Chung-liang Huang, Joyce Cary, William Barrett, Steven Jay Gould, Igor Stravinsky, R. D. Laing, Bo-In Lee, Kendra Crossen, E. L. Doctorow, Rembrandt Van Rijn, John Berryman, Fritjof Capra, Candice Hahn, Carl Jung, Gary Coward, Lewis Thomas, Philip Guston, Merce Cunningham, Van Morrison, Claude Monet, Gertrude Stein, Rollo May, Richard Strauss, M. C. Richards, Otis Redding, Viktor Lowenfeld . . .

Thank you.

No More Secondhand Art

Introduction

Some years ago, as a graduate student studying painting and art history at a major university, I and some fellow students attended an exhibition held at our school of the drawings and paintings of a group of highly respected art historians. All of these gentlemen were outstanding scholars in their respective fields of art history. They were not only scholars of ancient and medieval periods but experts as well on contemporary style, known for the depth of knowledge and sensitivity with which they wrote and lectured on the historical contexts of artist, period, style, and antecedents. They saw subtleties of meaning in iconography and nuances in formal elements. These men could discriminate between an authentic work and a fraud on the basis of the merest detail of brush stroke, confidence in line quality, or palette usage. They were able aestheticians, outspoken and eloquent art critics. Allowing for even a modicum of technical training and manual dexterity, great things, we felt, must come forth from men such as these.

We thus entered the gallery with high expectations. We had listened to these erudite men for months and had marveled as they pointed out details of order and craft that would have gone undetected by lesser observers. With a firm sense of their own powers of observation they had cleverly, and with good humor, indicated the moments of naiveté and awkwardness in Van Gogh and Cezanne, the lapses of good taste in Rubens, the charming and endearing primitiveness of Duccio and Pisanello. What greatness, we thought, must come from these great minds!

The atmosphere in the gallery was cool and reserved. The works resembled all that was best in Western art. In fact, the exhibition resembled nothing so much as a condensed Western Art survey course. Every canon of good form, every detail of craft was in clear evidence. The iconography used was subtle and complex and the themes profound. The compositions were taut; nothing was superfluous, nothing missing. The landscapes, still lifes, and portraits depicted all that is thought beautiful. The symbols and classical allusions were erudite and cleverly employed. Beyond doubt, the entire exhibition hall had the unmistakable feel to it of a sanctuary of learning and of beauty. We walked through the show, scrutinizing the works with ever slower and heavier tread, and came away quiet and joyless, as if life had been somehow drained from us. Why?

Here were paintings that obeyed every principle of good form derived from the grandest of masters: Bellini, Rubens, Ingres, Cezanne, Pissaro, De Chirico. Yet these works cast such a different light and elicited such a different, diminished reaction. There was no vitality here, no direct engagement with life, with its mind- and soul-slamming mysteries. These were timid and bookish things, devoid of the poignant urgency of a life lived in fullness and intimacy. It was secondhand art. We left the gallery stunned and saddened, disoriented. How could the best of the best and the brightest be so tedious, so empty, so dead?

Why is it that dexterity, knowledge of art, and taste do not necessarily add up to what we seek in art? What ingredient is missing whose presence would make the work throb with vitality and invite us to live more fully—or at least to *see* more fully—as a consequence?

This is not at all to say that dexterity, knowledge, and taste are unnecessary components of art that *does* move us. It is to say that they are insufficient in themselves and that other qualities of mind and spirit must be present for these constituents to spill over into an art with the power to move us to tears, laughter, or silence.

Unless a courageous stance to life is coupled with these ingredients, tedious and shallow things will be made. Unless a capacity to dream and fantasize is there, derivative things will be made. Without an unflinching sense of self, the work will ring hollow and will remain unconvincing. Unless one wanders into territory that is perplexing, mysterious, overwhelming, the work will be pedestrian and predictable, and so will we. To cultivate these "other" constituents of art and life, and so improve one's life, and consequently one's art, the creative encounter must be discovered and employed.

The making and teaching of much art today is a fraudulent affair, devoid of large, deep purposes. Art today seems primarily in the service of decoration, innovation, or self-expression. At the same time, we seem to have lost contact with the earlier, more profound functions of art, which have always had to do with personal and collective empowerment, personal growth, communion with this world, and the search for what lies beneath and above this world.

In pursuing a vital confrontation with life and our own creativity, we are not interested in putting art and ourselves in the service of pretty things or novel things, or even in the mere exposure of ourselves. We want to reclaim the actual power of art. Through the creative encounter we seek to facilitate our private and communal evolution so that we may become who we prefer to be.

Some years ago, in a book he called *No More Secondhand God,* Buckminster Fuller said something like this: Why not meet God directly? Why take someone else's story about hearing someone else's story as your own religious experience? If you are inclined to meet God, why not go out and look the fellow up? Why take someone else's word for what God is like? Why not be the first Christian, the first Jew?

In just this same way, we can engage in the creative process with the awe and exhilaration of every new beginning, and we can even from time to time do so without the heavy presence of precedent binding our hands and blinding our eyes with the accomplishments of others.

In order for us to engage in image making with the fullness of power that this primary act of creation has to offer, we must remove the barrier that otherwise keeps us at a harmless distance from any authentic creative encounter. This barrier may be characterized as a densely woven thicket of everything we have ever been told about art. If we are to engage in the act of creation directly and fully, we must set aside all that is secondhand news and bear witness to our direct encounter with the world as if for the first time. Putting aside our personal history, as heroic an effort as that may require, is an essential first step toward uncovering our original selves. Allowing our past to assert itself at the outset in our present will only cause our past to re-create itself in the present, to issue just another edition of who we were, or already are. At the same time, we must put aside—even for a moment—the memory of every picture we have ever seen, of every art history course and art book, of every TV special on Picasso or Pollack, of every art teacher, art lesson and art kit. Art history is, after all, someone else's story about someone else's adventures. If we can set aside art's history for a moment we might allow ourselves to see past our inheritance of images and ideas of places we have never been to and people we have never met. If we can do this, however briefly, we may be able to stop tricking ourselves into believing that just because we saw a spread of photos in *National Geographic* we know anything about the people of, say, Kurdistan. In truth, we don't know anything about the people of Kurdistan. What we do know are some three-by-five-inch pictures in a nine-by-eleven-inch magazine lying on our living room table. And that is not Kurdistan.

By the same token, we really do not know anything about Rembrandt, Tintaretto, the Renaissance, classical Greece, Jackson Pollack, or Matisse. All we know are stories, secondhand stories of other people and other times. In fact, the stories we know were written by people who themselves only read other people's stories. Pale and distorted hand-me-downs—interesting and entertaining, perhaps, but not to be taken as truth, certainly not as primary reality.

A few artifacts of the primary luminaries are left to us, but even these remnants are rarely examined face to face. The prints and pictures in coffee-table books, the slides that we study in darkened rooms come to us as painfully scaled-down images stapled to some erudite commentary provided by an academician whose mind is totally dissimilar to our own and whose eyes certainly never saw the artists at work in their studios.

No matter how rich the legacy, all this secondhand stuff gets in the way of picking up a lump of clay and squeezing life-force into it, being in awe of ourselves as a genuine creative force in the universe, having magic in our hands, fashioning a new world that awaits our presence to bring it forward. For this kind of real experience, we need to draw from within.

I

Drawing from Within: Rediscovering the Transformative Powers of Art

THE CREATIVE ENTERPRISE AS A JOURNEY

How breathtaking it is to start out on a journey into the unknown. How much easier, more comfortable, and reassuring it is to stay where we are among familiar faces and places. Even if where we presently are is not all that we would prefer, it is at least known. That in itself is somehow comforting. To start off in new directions—about to encounter who knows what, at risk of the way becoming confused at any point—takes courage. Or, to use a better word, faith. Faith that even when there are no external signs to indicate where and how we should proceed, we are not yet lost.

Setting out on that journey in the hope of uncovering sources of inner worth so that we may step more lightly and confidently through life is our ultimate goal; our means will be the creative act.

Suppose life *is* a journey, an endless, surprising odyssey in which we may move from naiveté to wisdom, from self-consciousness and awkwardness to grace, and from superficial knowledge to profound wonder. The infinite menu of possibilities that life continuously displays before us may be viewed as an invitation to embark on this adventure through varied and unpredictable terrain. The artistic process is more than a collection of crafted things; it is more than the process of creating those things. It is the chance to encounter dimensions of our inner being and to discover deep, rewarding patterns of meaning.

There comes a time in the forging of imagery when we run out of ideas, run thin on the courage necessary to push beyond the known and ordinary. Most often at this point of having exhausted our known complement of resources, we give up the task and retreat to surer ground. But for those who stay in the creative arena during this anxious period, who do not fall back, there sometimes comes a sudden infusion of energy and clarity. It's as if we were suddenly joined by a hidden ally that carries us past our usual insuffi-

ciencies and toward uncharted heights and depths. The releasing of this secret sharer, seemingly unbounded by constraints of time and space, is a
major, perhaps *the* major, reward of the creative engagement. Making the
acquaintance of this ally will be a major purpose of our quest.

BEYOND BEAUTY AND NOVELTY

Try following a train of thought with me. Let's explore the suggestion that
what we currently take to be the purposes of art differ vastly from the original intentions of the world's ancient and contemporary primal peoples. Suppose that for these people the making of what we now call art actually con-
stituted the most important societal activity besides—or even before—
one's basic everyday tasks for the maintenance of life. And suppose these
artifacts were made not, as in our modern society, for mere decoration or
for the gratification of self-expression, but as powerful and instrumental vehicles of personal and collective transformation. (By "transformation" I
mean changing the quality of life from its current condition to a preferred
and elevated one.) If art, then or now, were to be in the service of transforming the individual and the society, it would serve in these ways:
- Renewing and reaffirming the covenants between humankind and nature and between man and God
- Grappling with the ephemeral qualities of life and with our own
mortality
- Marking significant times, places, and events
- Celebrating the gifts of life
- Fulfilling individual potentialities and collective possibilities
- Discovering the actual range of human possibilities
- Awakening us to higher levels of consciousness

Now imagine that nothing remained of these ancient people but the durable artifacts that were employed in these transformational practices. Being
made of more perishable stuff, other and more revealing artifacts of these
people—such as their beliefs, language, ceremonies, oral histories, ideas,
values, and myths—would have all vanished with the last member of that
civilization. Embedded though they once were in a complex of beliefs and
intentions, only the bare artifacts remain: crowns, staffs, icons, maces,
swords. These objects, these formed things now stripped bare of their mys-
tic meanings and their designated purposes, are what we now uncover and
examine.

The objects possess the poignancy of a bereft child—or rather, they attack our sense of well-being in the same way. We may not know the specific

cause of the cry, but nonetheless we are moved by its heartrending sincerity and fullness of expression. We gaze at a knife in our hands, innocent of the terrible powers this same object possessed for its original owners. We pick up and admire the aesthetics of the blade's keen edge, a blade that may have passed through human hearts. We marvel at its symmetry, the fine, even cadence of its serrations, still intact after so many years, after so much use.

Our aesthetic sensibilities are delighted by the mace, the crown, the staff in the showcase, and we cannot help our oblivion to the gods, goddesses, demons, and spirits who swarmed around these same objects in other times and other places.

Thus moved by form and finish, we declare these sacred instruments to be merely beautiful, and we give their makers a title from our own list of occupations: artists. No matter that the makers of these objects in no way resembled or thought of themselves as what we would call artists. No matter that the purposes these objects served in no way resemble the purposes we now make art serve. We call this work art and we call their makers artists, caring little that they called their work prayer and their makers shamans or devotees or historians or celebrants or healers or prophets.

Because we live in a secular, mechanistic world, we take these artifacts equally to be secular undertakings and mechanical things. And we must ask ourselves: Can a people as devoid of spiritual imagination and experience as we are ever know about the original purposes of artifacts made by people for whom the whole universe was/is sacred?

We turn amulets into trinkets, powerful medicine into "collectibles," holy myths into quaint folk-tales. We marvel at the care and dexterity, the tastefulness exhibited in the artifacts of ancient and primal artisans. We admire those qualities of coherence and finish in their manufacture, and we declare them beautiful. For us, craft is in the service of beauty, and beauty is one of the qualities of an a priori higher "good."

For the primal image-maker, craft was not in the service of beauty in and of itself. Instead, craft was in the service of power. The more carefully wrought the object was, the more powerfully the object would serve as an instrument of transformation and the more likely the gods would be inclined to honor the supplication.

Why would the gods look more favorably upon things cared for and highly crafted? Here we must be speculative. A fair guess as to the thinking, not of the gods, but of those who believe they know the tastes of gods, is that the more carefully an object was made, the more the object resembled the ways of the gods themselves, and how they make things. How do gods make things? Just look around. Exquisitely. Every particle of the universe exquisitely fits in and to every other particle. Every leaf, stone, frog, fingernail and feather is intricately fashioned with not a thing left over, not a thing left out, and all with symmetry, delicacy, and power. This is the way of the gods; this is the way of the creation. Things made for the gods must employ these same criteria of goodness if they are going to be acceptable to these gods.

Just as sunsets, sunflowers, the seasons, and babies are exact, albeit passing, harmonies that yield gracefully as they move from one phase into the next, so must each feature of the mask, crown, mace, cape, gesture, and beat be exact: full of grace and economy, purposeful, and fitted to what preceded it and what will follow. Beauty was not the intended outcome. Beauty was a natural by-product of craft diligently applied to serious things.

Unaware of the original intentions of craft, we have taken the by-product of art, beauty, as the ultimate good of art. This misreading of the intention of art and the necessary care given to its formation, has, I believe, led us down a road full of sound and fury and yes, beauty—but what it all signifies is not at all certain.

The larger concepts of the authority of art held by primal people, as cited above, are not irretrievably lost to us today. These are not conceptions or practices belonging only to the distant past or far-off places. In fact, art as a search for personal and collective power and well-being is still held as central for most primal people, for Indigenous Americans as well as a small minority of the general community of artists. Jamake Highwater, in *The Primal Mind,* a revealing book on the conceptions of reality and the functions of the arts held by Indigenous Americans, is worth quoting at length on this subject.

For Indigenous Americans operating out of their original worldview, the arts are sources of power with which to do real and important business.

> Much of the "art" of American Indians is not art in the formal Western sense at all, but the careful representation of the iconography given to a person during a vision quest, or given in the dreams of later life. These emblems and images are materialized and used in pottery, textile, paintings, and carvings. Whether tribally or individually owned, the power of these images is what makes them significant and not simply their aesthetic impact upon those who do not know or understand the metaphor underlying their imagery. It is here, in this emblematic and visionary realm, that all art of the world finally possesses its vividness and power. We have reconstructed the vision implicit in art as an image conforming to the norms of our cultures, mindless of the fact that we have thus transformed a ritualistic experience into something called "art" in an effort to convey an unspeakable revelation within the confines of our closed concept of reality. As a vision often divorced from its motivating power, decorative art is a dubious achievement.[1]

An image, a dance step, a song may function from time to time as enter-tainment, but the root and full practice of the arts lies in the recognition that art is power, an instrument of communion between the self and all that is important, all that is sacred. Where we usually assign the origin of the artist's imagery to the vague direction of intuition or creative play, or even creative problem-solving, a deeper source is cited and sought after by the Indige-nous American, as Highwater again indicates.

> The impulse behind Indian images has little concern for particularization and appearance. Even when the visions of individuals provide the iconography for the design painted upon pottery or woven into textile, still the imagery is vi-sionary rather than decorative or representational. Whether the paintings are the tribal icons of clans or the personally owned images of hunters, pottery-makers, or warriors, . . . in all of these instances the imagery remains spiritual in the purest sense of the term.
> Surely painters such as Kandinsky grasped much of the otherness of primal art and attempted within the bounds of Western interpretation to reinfuse their work with a nearly lost visionary power. Yet this discussion of "image" in the primal mentality has perhaps underscored the probability that much of the art produced by so-called Neo-Primitivists was a superficial reflection of the sur-face of primal imagery (a kind of plagiarism of appearances), rather than a real-ization of its underlying reality as the evocation of human dream and memory.[2]

In the history of European-based art, we too have a long tradition of be-lieving there must be some extranatural source for the visions of artists. The divine Muses of the Greeks, divine inspirations, even episodes of divine madness have played a role in the myth of the artist throughout our own history. But it is childish and quaint to speak of such things today as sources for art. We believe we have better evidence with which to assign cause to the imagery portrayed by our artists. We claim this is a mechanistic uni-verse, that all things and events owe their nature to various elaborations of things bumping into other things. Who knows? It may be so. But it is rather cold and lonely and haphazard out in the mechanistic conception of reality.

The cosmology of primal peoples is utterly different from this view. Theirs is not a dead, purposeless universe; the artist (and indeed everyone and everything else) is purposefully alive. As Highwater states,

> the individual experience of images and ideas is for almost all Indians of the Americas a communion with the "mighty something" that is the abiding power of the cosmos. Much as all creative people depend upon intuition or inspiration for their life-supporting and life-affirming discoveries and imaginings, Indians depend upon some sort of personal contact with the ineffable for their most precious wisdom.[3]

And the purpose of this wisdom? The purpose of these images, the essential function of art? First, it is to become personally enlightened, wise, and whole. Then, and as a consequence of the former function, the purpose of this wisdom, the purpose of art, is to make the community enlightened, wise, and whole.

The seeking after "wisdom" was the seeking after visions. Seeking after visions—isn't that what all artists do? It is, of course, but the source and functions of those visions are held to be very different things for us. For Indigenous Americans, Highwater says,

> in the initiation from childhood to maturity, no experience is as important . . . as the gaining of a spirit helper in a vision quest. Without it a person would surely fail in every major activity of life. So Indians do not usually await the appearance of some aspect of the *orenda* [a spiritual guide], but actively seek it. This is the basis of the vision quest. . . .
>
> In the old days, a young person traveled to some remote area where it was known that many powers dwelled—often a mountaintop, or the shore of a remote lake, sometimes in the depths of a deep forest. There the youth remained for several days and nights, alone and in utter silence, fasting from both food and water, humbly naked except for a loincloth since for most Indians the body is all a person owns. . . .

When returning to his or her people, the youth would describe the experience to close friends and relations, reconstructing it and filling in gaps, adapting it to the mythic norms of the culture. Often the vision, the songs, and the images given to the neophyte were kept secret for a lifetime, until, in old age, they were passed along to a deserving apprentice or to someone who was luckless enough not to have ever experienced a vision of his or her own. Even today successful visions support people for their entire lives. It is a power upon which they can call for guidance and courage.[4]

We need not hold to the Indian cosmology if that is inconsistent with our own. We needn't go off into the forests and wait for signs and voices in order to transpose the function of art from decoration and the pursuit of only beauty to art as the pursuit of empowerment, wisdom, and wholeness. Empowerment, wisdom, and wholeness are not intrinsic only to Indian views of reality and practice. These are values which we hold just as dear, if not sacred. Why not make them the primary purposes of our art? Why can't we have both decoration and wisdom, beauty and wholeness?

Joseph Zinker, an artist and therapist, in his book *Creative Process in Gestalt Therapy,* says this:

> Art is prayer—not the vulgarized notations handed down to us in the scriptures, but a fresh vital discovery of one's own special presence in the world. Marc Chagall was once asked if he attended a synagogue; he answered that his work is prayer.
>
> In the process of making anything, a person not only illuminates and illustrates his inner life, but moves beyond personal expression to make something which stands by itself. The work acquires its own internal validity, its own integrity. It is in this process of making something which stands on its own integral structure that the creator contacts a concrete reality outside his subjective life and moves into the realm of the transcendent.[5]

Our current conceptions of what art is and what it does seem such pale dilutions of what could be. Perhaps we have misread the signs. Perhaps we are heading off into territory that, although picturesque, offers little other than entertainment.

As a result we have millions of earnest people in thousands of schools scrubbing away, rubbing, squeezing, madly polishing things in the hopes of forming the "beautiful thing." Most do not. Some diligent, gifted few do end up making beautiful things to grace homes and offices, and have their moment of glory. But I suspect many such artisans eventually realize that the goal they so desperately sought and paid such a high price for, rings hollow. If it has been mere beauty they sought after, merely the well-formed thing, a certain vague sense of incompleteness pervades their sense of self. I think the same can be said about those who seek merely the novel thing. Beauty and novelty alike provide the maker and the receiver with an immediate shock and reward to the senses. But then what? What is left to muse upon, to grow with, to satisfy the deeper needs of the spirit?

And what of all those who toil after beauty and novelty and fail to achieve even this? Their fate seems to be to persist in throwing themselves again and again into the same shallow enterprise. They take class after class, stare at bevies of naked models, piles of glass vases stuffed with meadows of silk and real flowers. They drag themselves out in all weather to catch that touching light as it glints on crests of waves, pouting waifs' cheeks, dew-moistened poppies. They worry over foreshortenings of legs and noses. They read and reread Jansen's history of art, staying up half the night to get the dates, names, and styles to align themselves in proper order. All this in the service of preparing themselves to make beautiful things, unique things.

The trophy for all this labor? Some nice-looking objects, some not so nice. Could this possibly be what it is all about?

If art is much more than beauty and novelty, if it is truly to be a source of renewal, a celebration of life, a means of awakening, we have to start rethinking the whole creative enterprise.

INSIDE, NOT OUT

It is ironic that our very concept of art, and what is required to make it, dooms most would-be artists to frustration and modest results. There are three false and killing notions about art. The first is that art is about beauty. The second is that in order to be an artist you must train your hand to be dexterous and your eye to be accurate. The third is that there are certain canons of good form that if applied, will bring about beautiful things. Each of these three precepts is true, but none is true enough. Their perversity resides in their incompleteness, not in their wrongness.

Each of these characteristics has a correlate dimension that, if given close attention, can bring about enterprises of substantial worth for both the artist and the public. The correlate of "art as beauty" is "art as meaning." The correlate of a prepared hand and eye is a prepared heart, mind, and spirit. The correlate of the formulas of good design is the *absence* of any formula, where imagination serves as a better guide than memory, and where courage fuels the journey from the known to the unknown.

It seems to me that I make shallow and uninteresting things whenever I challenge myself to do shallow and uninteresting tasks. We see a haystack by Monet, an iris by Van Gogh, or an asparagus spear by Manet and marvel at their presence and spirit and think that these works were about haystacks, irises, and asparagus. Not at all! Monet, Van Gogh, Manet *employed* haystacks, irises, asparagus to speak of the symphonies of light, the glory of God's creations, the life force residing in all form. We care about those paintings more than we care about stacks of hay, flowers, and vegetables because we care more about light, God, and life than we do about any of their particular manifestations. *Meaning,* not beauty, is what we are after. Big, deep, wide meaning.

The mistake we make is to take the particular form that the response to the challenge takes, for the challenge itself. Instead of preparing ourselves to first raise and then confront the question, we prepare ourselves to make renditions of someone else's answers. Once we have managed to mimic another artist or nature's look, what will we have gained? Mindless copies. Is that what the world needs? Paint squished about to resemble apples, crockery, sunsets? Don't we have enough apples as it is? Isn't one sunset a day sufficient? Is it too much a bother to go to the window and see the sun set? Must we stick a copy of it on our wall, trivialize it, miniaturize it so that it will forever set docilely above our tidy couch?

What we never get enough of is *meaning.* What *does* all this mean? Why *are* we here? Where are we going? Who am I? How do I fit into this unspeakable universe? Are we alone? What shall I do with my passions, my loneliness, my possibilities? How can I ever say "Thank you" enough for all this? Why me? Why them? How could all this happen? Is there a pattern to this boundless garment? Who's running this operation? Why? These are the questions that animate artists to spin and jump and howl until the right way is found to address the big conundrum that both invites and confounds our imagination.

What about techniques and formulas? Where do they fit in the education of the artist? All art schools and art books (with rare exceptions) base their methods for the formation of the artist on shaping the technical and theoretical tools for good form. No need for more of this here. A list of books that do provide a thorough treatment of the skills of drawing follows:

A Contemporary Approach to Drawing by Claudia Betti and Teel Sale (New York: Holt, Rinehart & Winston, 1980)
The Art of Drawing by Bernard Chast, 3rd ed. (New York: Holt, Rinehart & Winston, 1983)

The Art of Responsive Drawing by Nathan Goldstein, 2nd ed. (Englewood Cliffs, N.J.: Prentice-Hall, 1977)

A Guide to Drawing by Daniel M. Mendelowitz and Duane A. Wakeham, 4th ed. (New York: Holt, Rinehart & Winston, 1988)

The Craft of Drawing: A Handbook of Materials and Techniques by Dan Wood (Orlando, Fla.: Harcourt Brace Jovanovich, 1988)

The Natural Way to Draw: A Working Plan for Art Study by Kimon Nicolaidis (Boston: Houghton Mifflin, 1941)

Of course technique is important; so are principles of design. But you already know this. You also know what it takes to acquire these traits: long, hard work. Do you want to draw like Rembrandt or Degas? Simple! Just draw ten hours a day, six days a week for forty years. That's how they did it. Ready for that? How did Monet paint those densely woven symphonies of strokes of light, weaving that luminescent Japanese bridge over that swarming lily pond? First he excavated a huge hole, then diverted a river to fill the hole, planted it with lily pads, then built a Japanese bridge over the whole thing, all at vast expense. Then he bought a boat, made a floating studio out of it and for twelve hours a day, for over twenty years, he paddled around that pond, and painted and painted until his eyes glazed over. If you want to make stuff that has Monet's charm, have Monet's passion, devotion, largesse, sacrifice.

The techniques of Monet or Degas can be copied; their principles of design are not obscure, they can be learned. If you want them for yourself, you can have them—for a price. And the price is dearer than you may think. Not only will you have to put in at least as much time as they did in developing these same skills, all your living days, but the real price you will have paid is that you will have succeeded in becoming *them,* and will have missed becoming *you.*

Monet's technique and principles of design *are* Monet. They were created by him so that he could portray what he alone was seeing and thinking and feeling. These are not simply techniques or principles of design. They are conceptions of the world. Monet had to create his own repertoire of techniques and principles of design because he could not portray through the prevailing means what he alone was seeing and feeling. You can't have his technique or apply his principles of design without becoming him. Would you really experience the life that Rembrandt did, the untimely loss of all your loved ones, the loss of all his earthly possessions, the fall from grace and good fortune? Would you really experience the life Van Gogh had to suffer? Are you willing to pay that price—even if you could—just to paint some irises and sunflowers?

Better to raise the questions Monet did than to mimic his responses. What are his questions, the task he set himself? They are remarkably similar to the questions any artist, any creative person, any awake person asks. "What is that damn thing out there? What does an idea look like? How can I give form to a feeling? How does this whole mess fit together? How can I speak about the thing no longer there? The thing not here yet? Why am I moved like this by mere daylight, by nightfall? Is there truth here, or merely beauty? Does this line have integrity, or is it guile? What have I made up, what have I observed? Of all the things I can do, what shall I do, what should I do? Will I ever get it right?"

Your particular techniques and your principles of design will be derived from your struggle with these questions. Monet did it. Rembrandt did it. So did Bellini, Breughel, Bosch, Bach, Brahms, Beethoven, Byron, Bartók, Berlioz, Bernstein, Brubeck, Basie, Balanchine, Beckett, Bergman, Beckmann, Berryman, Borges, Bellow, Baldwin. You get the picture.

The bite of the quest is what invigorates the artist to be equal to the task of craft and order. The solutions to the problems posed in art do not lie outside in the realms of technique and formula; they reside in the realm of fresh thinking about perennial issues, in honest feelings and awakened spirit.

All creative journeys begin with a challenge to introspection, to fathom not only "what's out there," but "what's in here." They are invitations to original response much as the student of Zen is confronted with a koan. Seeking the ordinary response, the pat and the past resolution may achieve a decent result but will most likely be of little transformative value. Illustrating a preconception keeps our hand slave to a mind that is already intent on its goals and means. Responses drawn from our standing repertoire of answers will only reinforce the person we already are, which more than likely is much like the person we were. Which is nice for the reassurance that memory brings, but provides little force by which to gain the high ground of an expanded future.

So, dear reader, do not set stock in correct responses, in familiar ways, or in the ways of others. This is a time of trusting hand and heart to find their way. Allow the mind to follow—not lead—the hand. Most often the eyes are the windows of the mind, bringing in evidence to that seat of judgment for a verdict. Train your eyes instead to be passive observers of the activity of your hands. Allow the body to monitor the rightness of the stroke and the poignancy of the emergent image. You will know when some novel image or gesture is "right," because your body will register a sense of well-being, naturalness, quiet strength.

Does this mean that as artists we are compelled to seek novel ways to address timeless issues? Is originality the requirement of art? Not at all. What

is required is freshness. Originality may be the darling of the fans of art, but it is hardly the ambition of artists of serious intent. When what needs saying can be said best with available material, we use it. Why not? When the thing needing expression can't be caught with conventional apparatus, we invent our own. Why not?

Originality is a false issue, and so is technique. As important as these two factors are, they are impediments only to those who stand outside of art. Inside, the creative experience is quite different. Inside is inquiry, the expansion of emotional depth and range, the tuning of the spirit, and the quest for meaning.

We regard originality in the arts as a special good—as if it were a good in itself. It is not. We think artists cavalierly abandon convention to indulge their private reveries. They do not. On the contrary, artists are people who are driven to invent new terms to portray new ideas, ideas whose shape cannot be expressed by the stock language of old ideas. The need that drives artists outside of convention's bounds is not originality for its own sake, but the desire to share what is known, apparently, only to oneself, and to shape utterance, gesture, and sign so as to carry that meaning out from the interior of self and into the public domain. The price of this necessary private way of speaking is often isolation, a blank stare in return for a heartfelt reaching out, silence in return for a song.

But what is to be done? You—the artist—do see the world in a way that no one else does. Will you diminish that vision, blunt its edges by presenting it to yourself as well as to the world through off-the-rack terms not of your design? Most of us do. It's easier. And, in truth, our language *is* marvelously flexible, able to represent enormous ranges and subtleties of meanings. In the main it does what needs doing. But not always.

It is at those moments—when what you know and feel resides in no available form—that you are presented with an exquisite choice. You may turn away from that original experience, letting it die for lack of being given palpable form, or you may choose to stay with the original experience, as you try and try again to discover metaphors to yield up the meaning of that experience. Having created a metaphor within which your meaning resides, you have made that thing called art. In your uniqueness, you have also extended the vocabulary of art by representing for the first time another view of the world. Not gratuitously, not as an egotistic display of talents do you seek to be original or creative. You did what you had to do to bear witness to the things you know. That's all. That's *All.*

TOWARD MEANING, NOT BEAUTY

The pursuit of the beautiful holds such an ancient and venerable position in the arts that we often fail to notice the inherent limitations of this notion and the price it exacts from practitioners and viewers alike.

The most obvious problem with making art synonymous with beauty is that they really are two distinct terms referring to two entirely different objectives. The term *art* refers to a category of human activity. The term *beauty* refers to a quality of human activity, natural objects, and events. Art is the making of expressive symbols, something all humans do spontaneously and for the most part effortlessly. In contrast to the natural ease of image making, the making of beautiful objects requires a level of skill and knowledge that only the few ever exhibit. Therein lies the problem: so few people who attempt to capture the beautiful ever do so. Beauty is cherished in part because it is so rare, so difficult to achieve, and so elusive. The necessary rarity of beauty causes the few to be elevated, the many to be intimidated, jealous, and too often demeaned. For every winner in the beauty contests of art and life there are legions of losers, second-rates, honorable and not-so-honorable mentions. The inherent difficulty of approaching the beautiful causes trepidation for most people willing to engage in art, and trepidation can't help but inhibit full expression.

Beauty derives its status from a comparison of two or more entities. These entities are necessarily unequal, and one must conform to a third and external standard more closely than the other; it is against this third standard that they will be judged. The contestant closest to this external mark is more "beautiful" than the other. The one farthest from the standard is deemed less beautiful, somewhat defective, deficient. The farther from the mark one is, the more inherently defective one takes oneself as being—and the more alienated one becomes from the enterprise. This alienation serves in turn to bring about a hesitant approach to both art and life. A creative endeavor in which the outcome is likely to end up disastrously for the participant is an undertaking that seems far from inviting. It may well be that for just this reason so few do accept the open invitation to create, discover, awake.

Yet art has traditionally had another function besides the pursuit of beauty, one that is less costly; equally legitimate, ancient in origin, and universal in usage; and perhaps even more profound. I mean the pursuit of meaning. By shifting our concerns from trying to make the beautiful thing to seeking the honest and the meaningful thing, two critical objectives may be accomplished. First, the paralyzing self-consciousness that invariably accompanies the search for beauty is diminished. When we give up concern for making something beautiful we also drop any comparison of our work with external standards of excellence, and drop the feelings of ineptitude that inevitably result from such comparison. The pursuit of the merely decorative edge of beauty is thereby put into its appropriate place: nice if it is there, but structurally unessential.

In seeking the meaningful rather than the beautiful, we nurture an endeavor which lies at the deepest levels of the traditional function of art: the uniquely human quest for establishing personal meaning in a possibly meaningful universe. The psychotherapist and student of creativity Rollo May says of this process,

> The poet's labor is to struggle with the meaninglessness and silence of the world until he can force it to mean; until he can make the silence answer and the Non-being be.[6]

In speaking of Giacometti and the utter devotion that artist gave to finding ever more adequate ways to portray what demanded being said, May goes on to say:

> This challenge gave his life meaning. He and his kind seek to bring their own visions of what it means to be human, and to see through that vision to a world of reality, however ephemeral, however consistently that reality vanishes each time you concentrate on it.[7]

Our aim, then, would be to nurture the ability to find even more powerful means to investigate, represent, and share a sense of ourself and our place in the world with those who matter. This is a grander and more rewarding engagement with art than our conventional aim, the creation of highly crafted objects with which to allure and enchant. There is nothing wrong with allure and enchantment. We certainly have precious few moments of allure and enchantment in our lives. But they are not the whole purpose of art, for they do not ask what we wish to enchant, or whom (or what) we wish to lure. To illustrate this important distinction between an art serving in the pursuit of meaning and that in pursuit of beauty, we can turn to another art form: the dance. There was a time when dance was in the service of bringing about important things, in the service of appealing to the forces of the universe that determined our fate. Jamake Highwater describes this conception of the purpose of dance (and therefore of art) this way:

> . . . much of the white man's dancing . . . had greatly declined from its ritual purposes when contemporary dancers at the turn of the twentieth century began the arduous effort of rediscovering the potential of relating dancing to the most serious rather than the most superficial aspects of the human condition. But for primal peoples, dance perfectly and simultaneously embodies the most commonplace and the most exceptional ideals. If dance relates imperfectly to the contemporary world, it is perhaps because dance was so neglected during that long evolution and did not develop that kind of relationship to the white audience which it has always had in relation to primal cultures.[8]

In southern France, a folk dance called the *farandole* is still performed. It is a labyrinth-patterned dance common in much European folk choreography. Its patterns derive from an ancient symbol found on Greek coins.

The snakelike winding of the *farandole* . . . closely resembles a journey to the middle of the labyrinth. This Greek labyrinth pattern was a vision of the passage of a dead person to the land of the afterlife, a passage fraught with danger from evil powers. In performing a funeral dance toward the middle of a manmade labyrinth, the ancients were demonstrating that people possess the force to direct certain events of nature through sympathetic rites. This winding *farandole* was a means of mimicking the spirit of the dead person and helping it on its way. Today the farmers of Provence still perform the *farandole* but without any conscious purpose other than the enjoyment of music and movement. In this case, the expressive form of the ritual has been abandoned. What remains is neither art nor ritual but something else: an entertainment, a game.[9]

Seeking after meaningful and not merely beautiful objects will not result in the creation of a turbulence of gestures and marks as many fear it will. It does not lead to disregard for carefully made things; the effect, in fact, is quite the opposite. When we are motivated to find increasingly complete and satisfying means to convey what is of great personal importance, and draw from both the conscious and subconscious levels, our images naturally become more vivid, deeper, more articulate, and (interestingly!) somehow more universal. Relating how this realization was experienced personally, Rollo May states:

> . . . in the breakthrough of this insight . . . everything around me became suddenly vivid. . . . The moment the insight broke through, there was a special translucence that enveloped the world, and my vision was given a special clarity.[10]

Images made from this premise may sometimes lack a surface polish, but we miss this veneer no more so than we miss it in the work of Matisse, de Kooning or Van Gogh. What they may lack in politeness and sheen, they more than compensate for by their added sense of urgency, poignancy, self-confidence, and integrity.

The search for meaning is open-ended and exhilarating, if uncertain. Once we create imagery that honestly represents how life feels from the inside, there is a deep sense of personal empowerment and a new degree of private certainty as a result of having finally touched down to the original bedrock of our original self. Rollo May expresses the elation one feels of finding the right fit between the thing needing saying and the thing said in this fashion:

> There is a curiously sharp sense of joy—or perhaps better expressed, a sense of mild ecstasy—that comes when you find the particular form required by your creation.[11]

This is the stuff of art.

ON THE DIFFICULTY OF "CAPTURING LIFE"

Starting off by making a "picture" is like starting off composing a symphony. It's the most complex and difficult thing to do, and yet it is the very first task given a would-be student! In fact, most students wreck themselves on this first step by attempting to accomplish the most complex and difficult of all things an artist can be faced with: the making of an image that is supposed to look like the same thing in the world.

To replicate the world as it is given is an impossible undertaking, and so countless would-be artists dash themselves unwittingly on the harbor rocks before even getting underway. The fatal myth they have been led to believe is that art is about replicating beautiful things and moments of the world. They do not understand that no one can succeed in this killing task. No one.

Why? For many reasons. Because things in the world are in four dimensions (three of space and one of time), whereas images on planes (paper, canvas) are in two dimensions and are frozen in time; sculpture is in three dimensions of space but is equally frozen in time. Things in the world are biologically alive and somehow have soul, while images are not alive and have no soul. Things in the world are in constant motion, evolving, growing, dying; not even Michaelangelo can make his marble Madonna lift up her eyes from her son's mortally wounded body, and no aroma emanates from the wild sunflowers of Van Gogh. "Things" in the world are really not things

22

at all. They are living events, each the result of myriad local and distant forces of heat, light, wind, moisture, gravity, and history. The poignancy of that brilliant blaze of autumn scarlet erupting from a maple tree against the deep moody greens of a pine-dotted mountain rests in part on our knowledge that this is a precious moment, soon to be followed by sullen, gray days and bare winter limbs. Images don't evolve, they remain stubbornly as they are. Indeed, their power comes from their grand refusal to be budged.

We can't squash something down from four dimensions into two or three, something alive into something not alive, some event into some object, without eviscerating the thing, leaving out essential qualities of the original essence of the observed thing. The more we try to capture "the actual thing out there" the more glaring will be our ineptitude, the more embarrassingly short we fall, the less vitality the image has, and the more painfully dead and flat the imitation appears. We can't do it. And everybody who has been around for a while learns that lesson and abandons this impossible and, really, quite empty enterprise.

"It is absurd to think of artists simply as 'painting nature' as though they were only anachronistic photographers of trees and lakes and mountains," Rollo May says.

> For them, nature is a medium, a language by which they reveal their world. What genuine painters do is reveal the underlying psychological and spiritual conditions of their relationship to their world; thus in the works of a great painter we have a reflection of the emotional and spiritual condition of human beings in that period of history. If you wish to understand the psychological and spiritual temper of any historical period, you can do no better than to look long and searchingly at its art. For in the art the underlying spiritual meaning of the period is expressed directly in symbols. . . .
>
> The vision of the artist or the poet is the intermediate determinant between the subject (the person) and the objective pole (the world waiting-to-be). It

23

will be non-being until the poet's struggle brings forth an answering meaning. The greatness of a poem or a painting is not that it portrays the *thing* observed or experienced, but that it portrays the artist's or the poet's vision cued off by his encounter with the reality. Hence the poem or the painting is unique, original, never to be duplicated.[12]

Still another way of expressing the purpose of art not as the representation of the outer form of things, but as the presentation of the encounter of humankind with the inner dynamics of the animating forces of the world, is offered by Jamake Highwater. He begins with a revealing quote from Mikel Dufrenne.

> For the [primal person], truth does not lie in the insignificant appearances of the everyday world but in the great cosmic forces which course through this world, in the exemplary events recounted in myth and repeated in ritual, and in all that gives meaning to appearances rather than receiving it from them. The same can be said about the totem poles of the Haida Indians [of the Northwest Coast of America], the painted ancestors of the New Hebrides, or the bronze figures of the Steppes. Such works attempt to render the invisible visible." The artist has used his body—his cumulative sensory being—to transform something mysterious into something tangible.
>
> For Indians, images are a means of celebrating mystery and not a manner of explaining it. For Kandinsky art was essentially the same thing: "To speak of mystery in terms of mystery. Is that not content? Is that not the conscious or unconscious *purpose* of the compulsive urge to create?[13]

The lesson is: Don't try to "capture" nature. It's like trying to capture the stars, or a butterfly—we can grab the body, but then we are left with the corpse and not the butterfly. We can't capture the storm-tossed ocean by scooping up a jar of sea water. The ocean is the ocean only when it is *ocean-ing:* rolling with the wind, streaming with living things, pounding rocks, fracturing sunlight, blowing our hair. The stuff in the bottle is only salt water in a bottle. In the same way, we can't capture, we can't "have" the ocean by converting it into colored paints on a piece of nine-by-eleven-inch paper.

We can't "have" the ocean, we can't "have" any *thing*—but we can engage in relationships, we can enter into a closeness to others, the carefulness of which transforms us both. Illustrative of this act of encounter and engagement is the following passage by the Jewish philosopher Martin Buber. Notice how his depth of concern for the object of his beholding creates an arena of relationship that has now become the "world" in which both he and the tree now dwell.

> I CONSIDER A TREE.
>
> I can look on it as a picture: stiff column in a shock of light, or splash of green shot with the delicate blue and silver of the background.
>
> I can perceive it as movement: flowing veins on clinging, pressing pith, suck

of the roots, breathing of the leaves, ceaseless commerce with earth and air—and the obscure growth itself.

I can classify it in a species and study it as a type in its structure and mode of life.

I can subdue its actual presence and form so sternly that I recognize it only as an expression of law—of the laws in accordance with which a constant opposition of forces is continually adjusted, or of those in accordance with which the component substances mingle and separate.

I can dissipate it and perpetuate it in number, in pure numerical relation.

In all this the tree remains my object, occupies space and time, and has its nature and constitution.

It can, however, also come about, if I have both will and grace, that in considering the tree I become bound up in relation to it. The tree is now no longer *It*. I have been seized by the power of exclusiveness.

To effect this it is not necessary for me to give up any of the ways in which I consider the tree. There is nothing from which I would have to turn my eyes away in order to see, and no knowledge that I would have to forget. Rather is everything, picture and movement, species and type, law and number, indivisibly united in this event.

Everything belonging to the tree is in this: its form and structure, its colors and chemical composition, its intercourse with the elements and with the stars, are all present in a single whole.

The tree is no impression, no play of my imagination, no value depending on my mood; but it is bodied over against me and has to do with me, as I with it—only in a different way.

Let no attempt be made to sap the strength from the meaning of the relation: relation is mutual.[14]

What can we do when we are moved by the tree, (the dusk, a handsome face, a field of wild flowers, the ocean)? If we are moved by the ocean, then we must move like the ocean. We must allow our hand to move across the surface of the page as the ocean moves across the sea bed. A heaving, ponderous sea—a heaving, ponderous gesture—a heaving, ponderous line. A deep and quiet mood descends upon us: a deep and quiet color in our hand. A certain softness in the air: a certain lightness in our stroke. A very simple and uncomplicated feeling of oneness with the moment: a simple range of colors and tones. A feeling of walking along that deserted beach forever: a long and narrow composition. Just as the ocean at any moment is the resultant of local and distant impinging events, so we must allow ourselves to lean into our art materials and flow in a similar manner.

The waters of the world are blackened seas, ice-bound lakes, or bubbling brooks as a consequence of all the forces acting upon their special wateriness, likewise our creations are the result of all the events of our life that have made us *us*. What we are is what we do. How we put our life together

25

is how we put our paints together. As we press ourselves against or into the surface of our media, we leave our mark. To allow that movement to run its natural course until the experience is savored fully in the marks left behind is to offer the fullness of evidence of the experience. This is the basis of an expressive, articulate image. Not a dead replication of something alive, but an image that is personal, unique, drawn from within, made in homage to the world without.

EXITING AND REENTERING THE ORDINARY WORLD

What is the sense of trying to make scaled-down, flat, dead copies of the world as it is, when we already have the world as it is? And in living color. As I have said before, the experienced artist has long since given up this impossible and unnecessary task of trying to replicate nature. The real task of art is to create a new, a meta-reality, combining the world as received with the life of the mind. In order to create a new world we have to give up our hold on this world, even if just for a while. We cannot be fully in both worlds simultaneously. How can we loose the hold ordinary living has upon us so that we may begin to open up to the possibility of a larger, a new, an unknown universe? Much has been written on this vital issue; in fact, it is the subject of many meditative and religious practices. Here are a few, briefly described approaches to releasing our grip on the old, ordinary world.

Stop Looking.

Literally stop looking. Close your eyes and just go on automatic pilot. Your visual imagination will simply ooze images; notice them as they spontaneously emerge. Don't label them or identify them; just watch them pass into and out of your awareness. We are an endless and automatic font of unique and universal imagery. Stop working so hard to *force* it out. Instead, loose your hold on all the determinations, and allow what is already in there to stream out.

There is a lovely moment that occurs often as we slide into sleep, at the transitional zone between soggy wakefulness and near-sleep. If we are reading, the words seem to melt and transform themselves into antic images, or our mind invents exotic scenarios based only marginally on the actual story line and the author's intention. Parades of incomplete characters swarm this way and that. Nice stuff, if a bit disconcerting. Then full sleep draws us down to darker stuff and oblivion. Just so, when we loose the hold with which self-conscious perception glues us to the physical world, we allow that quality of mind that spontaneously generates imagery to do its work.

Relax.

What hasn't already been said about how to relax? Along with "how to" books on cooking, dieting, and redecorating, "how to relax" treatises seem to top the best-seller lists. The popularity of the issue perhaps only underscores its real and deep importance.

Unwrinkle yourself in the way you relax best: take a walk, meditate, have a cup of tea, read some poetry. Whatever unwrinkles you, do it. Look at the stars, weed the garden, rearrange your paint box, whatever. You *do* know how to relax yourself. What you need to do is give yourself the time, space, and permission to do it. There's the rub: can we grant ourselves permission to be relaxed in a frantically purposeful and responsible world? How about a cup of tea?

Play.

Play is an experiment without hypotheses. Try this: Combine stuff—any stuff, such as torn paper, scraps of wood, bits of cloth or string—unguided by reason, precedent, taste, or propriety. Disassemble things in the same fashion. Have no end in mind but the pleasure or simply pure energy of fancy to propel you on. Save nothing from this activity, honor nothing. See how long you can sustain simply toying with new combinations without settling down or converging on old norms. Choose colors, shapes, marks that you wouldn't be caught dead using; see what happens.

Once upon a time, when we were very young, every moment of our day and every item and event within it were novel. With no conceptual framework against which items were to be arranged, we toyed and played with everything. We combined ordinary things in extraordinary arrangements. We stuck things into scandalous places, we shattered things revered by others. We know better now, now we are tamed, trained in the ways of our elders. And much of that is to the good. But not all. If our hard-won sense of shared propriety has cost us our ability to see the world as if for the first time, if we have given up our ability to play, we will have lost the cutting edge of our creativity.

So, when it's safe, and there aren't any other adults around, play.

Lighten Up.

Don't take yourself (just here and just now) so deadly seriously. In the long run—the very long run—nothing really matters; or conversely and equally so, everything matters. In both cases our contributions in this universe full of stars, galaxies, supernovas, oceans, continents, billions of other humans,

zillions of other life forms and who knows what!—our contribution in the welter of all of this is really rather modest and very uncertain. We may be at the center of our perceived universe, but we are certainly not at the structural center of the whole shebang. The universe has a great deal of momentum, keeping it all together and spinning pretty much with the same overall complexion from one moment to the next. Grand things happen from time to time, glaciers come and go, mountains rise, continents sink, stars burst on the scene, others collapse. Yes, and the universe does move over a bit to accommodate the new and hums on. In all of this coming and going on the galactic level, we scrub away at our canvas, chip away at our block of stone, squeeze clay. They really are—at least at some level—quite funny, our doings. So why not, from time to time, when the minutiae of life gets us down, why not look up at the stars—and laugh?

Change Your Pace.

Unless you periodically unbind yourself from the world as it is given to you from moment to moment, you will fail to release those qualities of your mind that can generate images of the world as you would prefer it to be or the world as you declare it as being.

I've noticed that there is a direct correlation between the pace of my thinking and the kind and quality of the thoughts so generated. I don't mean pace simply as a function of speed, but pace as something a bit more complex, as pattern or rhythm. If I go about my day touching all the ordinary bases in the ordinary rhythm and duration, I tend to think about the events of the day, and about myself, in pretty ordinary ways. That is, what I thought about life today is just about what I thought about life yesterday.

If, however, I rush about one day, and am compelled to do twice as many

28

things in half the time, this speeding up of the "movie" allows me to notice emergent patterns that my usual pace has failed to make evident. The same is true when I slow down the pace. When walking along the beach at one-quarter the rate I usually do, whole new catalogues of things and events become apparent. Colors I never saw before appear, shapes I never saw in shells before, outlines of trees, textures of waves, rhythms of light glinting from the trio of water, wind, and sun. I think the same thing may be true for others.

Seeing a new world, thinking new thoughts may not require creating a whole new world or engineering a whole new you. These other dimensions of the world and of ourselves may surround us at every moment but be concealed behind the veil of our ordinary-mindedness. One way to lift that veil is to shift the pace with which we do business with life. Speeding up, slowing down, whatever.

Get Lost.

Often we fail to allow ourselves to loose our hold on ordinary reality for fear we might get stuck too far from home and not be able to find our way back. Maybe so; but my experience has been that ordinary reality and our sense of propriety pop back into focus all too readily. The fear of losing the thread of return dooms us to sticking pretty close to home. And that is a high price to pay, for this is a very big and a very surprising universe.

We all know the comforts of the familiar. The familiar is what has already been explored and made our own; playing back old movies of past achievements offers us reorientation and a much needed affirmation of self-worth in a hurly-burly world. But the news from the outer edges of our sense of self and awareness of the world is quite different from the local news. Different things happen "out there." The texture of life, its density, is not the same as that which we ordinarily experience. These far reaches of our personal reality are all things that lay beyond what we currently permit ourselves to imagine, in a territory we forbid ourselves to enter. This is the region of the universe that contains all that we keep ourselves from encountering. Here lie the exotic, the erotic, the forbidden fruits, the crazy, the trivial, the absurd, the impossible, the sinful, the childish, the foolish, the exorbitant.

No matter how far we push this forbidden zone from us, it still remains immediately adjacent to our acceptable zone. What I am offering for consideration is this: from time to time, let's permit ourselves to approach the gate we have so arduously constructed to separate what we know and value from what we don't know and don't value, and experience what it is like to be at the very frontier of our personal boundaries.

My experience has been when I give myself permission to journey to the edges of the boundaries that I have set for myself, my senses become more acute. I become more perceptive. I notice more, my mind speeds up. I generate more and different scenarios to make sense of these foreign things and events which inhabit this forbidden territory. Eventually I get a little frightened or disoriented and retreat to safer, more familiar domains. But to the extent that I did tarry at my permissable edge, to that same extent I carry back with me a greater appreciation of the actual infinity of the universe in contrast to the rather puny corner I have marked off as my own. And the exhilaration, the hybridization of being that comes as another consequence of this is vital stuff for me as an artist of things and of life.

It is not uncommon for artists to reach a point in their development where they realize that what they know and can do is less than what there is to know and could be doing. This phase comes not at the point where their work is failing and seems uncertain, but at those moments of apparent great confidence in expression and elegance of presentation. In other words, these boundary-breaking phases of an artist's development occur when one has full command of one's craft and has portrayed with completeness the domain of one's interest. In midstride, as it were, the artist seems to pause in the making of art. One often retreats from the public showing of one's work as one goes through a period of reconsideration. Not infrequently at this time, earlier work is reexamined, some of it painted over (as in the cases of Turner, Degas, and De Kooning), some of it destroyed (as in the cases of Monet and Rauschenberg). When the artist reemerges from this self-imposed retreat, the new work is usually characterized by an increase of energy and a striding in a distinctly new direction.

We see this abrupt change in the work of Paul Klee, who entered this boundary-breaking phase with a rather conventional realistic style and emerged with his dreamlike, almost childlike lyricism. Picasso experienced many phases of sudden growth, from his Blue Period with its maudlin, elongated forms and cool palette to his Rose Period, characterized by classical features, roundness and fullness of form, and an almost placid indifference to the earlier works' concern for social issues. Picasso's shift from his Neoclassic period to his various Cubist phases also exemplify this boundary-breaking characteristic.

We find this same leap past the conventional in the latter work of Claude Monet. His early water lily series up until 1910 was in general characterized by an ethereal light that suffused the entire space and that bathed the forms, coalescing their edges into a dense smoky mat. The compositions were stately and classic in proportion. Monet was at the height of his powers as a colorist, and his work, rejected earlier as wild, out of control, bizarre, and untutored, was now highly esteemed by the Republic of France.[15] The prime minister of France, Clemenceau, prevailed on Monet to paint a major series of paintings based upon the water lily theme, to be acquired by the Republic. The grand master of the Impressionists reluctantly agreed and began to work. But something interesting happened. Monet hesitated, started, stopped, and became dissatisfied with the work. It was a period when he found some of his past work not up to his current standards, and he painted over some, destroyed others. Out of this period of reconsideration, Monet emerged with a new, refreshed style. An eighty-year-old man in poor health, with failing eyesight, he emerged with work that astonishes us still with its vitality and originality. Long, sweeping strokes loaded with improbable colors replace the shorter, more controlled dabs of his earlier, more refined palette. The lily pond, which was seen from a comfortable distance in the former work, is now seen up close, so much so that we feel we must be wading in it. Trees, water, and sky, each of which formerly occupied its separate territory, are now woven together in scintillating patterns. Vines and tendrils become colored calligraphy dancing across the equally animated surface of water, itself laced with outrageous color combinations: chartreuse over lilac, vermilion cut with rose madder, aqua, bright orange. An eighty-year-old man striding brightly into new domains.

Philip Guston, one of the most sublime of the New York School of Abstract Expressionists, also went through a heroic phase of boundary breaking. In 1962, Guston had a retrospective at the Guggenheim Museum in New York. The show revealed an inexorable development over thirty years of painting, beginning with his early romantic realism and culminating in a rarefied, highly personal form of abstraction. The spiritual dimension, which was always an element of his work, present first in his figures, transposed its presence in his later work to wholly invented elemental marks. These late paintings were the epitome of elegance; they floated effortlessly above the incidents and turmoil of everyday life and seemed to refer to the grandest scale of human sensibility, not unlike the concerns of Wagner or Joyce. The exhibition was extremely well received and Guston's place as a modern master, after long years of marginal recognition and very modest sales, seemed assured. He had finally arrived.

But then there was a period of silence, of reconsideration. Later, as revealed in his writing and interviews, his doubts about the sufficiency of abstract and highly personal marks to explore and to convey tangible concerns about being a vulnerable person in a hard world began to surface.[16] He abandoned his long-sought-after and recent success and began again at the beginning. It was as if he asked himself, and for the very first time: What is art? What does it look like? How do you make it? What does it mean?

Finally in 1970, after several years of working out a new vocabulary of forms and dealing with new themes, he brought his paintings before the public. And it shocked us all. Here was this grand and elegant master of the esoteric, presenting himself, as Hilton Kramer of the *New York Times* mercilessly said, as "a Mandarin pretending to be a stumblebum."[17] The work indeed leaped so far beyond what we had come to expect and enjoy that there seemed to be no ready basis for comprehending it. What had happened to this elegant gentleman? His work now reeked of stale beer, cigarette butts, smelly shoes. Hooded figures, brutishly painted, peered ominously at the viewer, heavy boots heaped together, suffocating each other. Fat lines lumbered around stocky, plug-ugly forms. Accusing eyes, wet cigars, bent nails. Who had gone wrong—us or him?

We know now why he had to do this, to leave what was dear and make one more stab at getting closer to the truth as he understood it. He had become so good at making pictures, he forgot *why* he made pictures. And he wanted to know that, more than he wanted to simply make more pictures without knowing why.

The willingness to let it all go just at the moment of greatest achievement and start again at the beginning appears a reckless act from the outside, but from the inside, for a person of integrity, it is the only thing one can do. For what drives the artist forward is the quest not only to say it right, but to say it at all. Now almost ten years after his death, and in the midst of a resurgence of figurative painting, Guston's latter works continue to challenge us in their bravery and unblinking candor, challenging our personal sense of integrity, with theirs.

My own experiences as an artist, though more modest in distinction, traverse a similar path. For about a decade I had been working on a theme of portals and passageways. I was intrigued by the idea of simultaneously leaving one domain and entering the other. (I had recently been married, we moved to a new country, I taught in a new school, we had our first child, and it was the sixties.) I explored this theme in a variety of images, each time attempting to find an image that would fully portray what I experienced in this transitional period of my life. After some years the work seemed to focus on a particularly gratifying image, and I felt the work begin to ring true. That is, what I was seeking, I began to find. My ability to create work that represented a full and adequate response to my queries came more quickly and frequently. To boot, the work was critically well received.

I remember in particular completing one such painting in which all the elements I had struggled so long and hard for years to tame and put to my disposal finally fell into place. The resulting work simply glowed (at least for me) with self-sufficiency. Ten years earlier I had asked myself a question, and in this painting, I finally answered it. A cascade of feelings seemed to pour out of me as I looked long and hard at the piece. First relief, then quiet joy, satisfaction, a sense of well-being. Hard on the heels of these self-congratulations, however, came the deeply disquieting feeling of emptiness and disorientation. Now what? Was this all there was? Was this all I wished to become? Was there nothing else out there or in here? Achieving what I had sought after, saying everything I knew about that question I posed for myself some ten years earlier, caused me to become aware of just how confined the scope of that question was, and how local the territory I had explored and mapped. It was time to move on. But where?

My work had culminated in knowing what I set out to know. Now I had to begin again, and I set out in the direction of my not knowing. I had to wander away from the familiar, get lost, so that I might come upon larger domains. These were to be difficult but necessary times.

I decided early on, in this new phase of my work, to keep my work private for as long as necessary, and I did not show my work even to family or friends for at least a year. My task during this period was to uncover or discover deeper (higher?) levels of awareness expressible in imagery. My work would be a matter of private reflection, a series of experiments to see what lay under, over, and to all sides of where I currently was. And in the seclusion of my studio, hesitant, humble, but rock-solid work began to emerge. These initial marks were not art, and I didn't force them to be. I watched them arrive and I studied them. I left what I took to be "mistakes" intact, returning later to explore them in the hopes they might lead me to areas that I had previously closed off. Some of these images did lead me to strange and rewarding places, some did not.

To keep me moving on, I promised myself not to seek consolidation, meaning, or beauty. I wanted only to travel on and to see. I employed media that I had never used before, so that it would be new in my hand, and would not elicit a ready and familiar gesture or image. I used colors and color combinations that repelled me because I wanted to explore rather than avoid the regions of my revulsions. I worked with my eyes closed for whole days, guided only by what literally felt right for my fingers, wrists, arms, and torso. Later on I looked at these "somatic" drawings to see what, if any, correspondence there may have been between what my body recognized as "good" and the evaluation of my eyes. During this period I was strict with myself not to repeat an image, no matter how appealing that image may have been. I also resisted, as best and as long as I could, the temptation to make an awkward and alien image nice and familiar.

Slowly, in fits and spurts, the region that I was working in began to expand. The territory was not simply getting bigger, but it also seemed deeper and higher. I like to think it's still happening.

Thin-Slice It.

No matter how many times and how thin we slice it, in each slice the world reveals a different aspect of itself. But we do have to slice it! Slicing it means we have to actively be there to meet it, touch it, poke it, allow it to smack into us. Each time we look at the world differently we see a different dimension of it. If we look at it the same way, we notice the same thing every time. This impoverishment of seeing on *our* part we take for an impoverished world. And, of course, it isn't.

So if we are to fully enjoy the show we must keep changing our seat. We must look underneath things, look closely at things, look very slowly, gobble up lots of things, stay with one thing all day, try impossible things. Sometimes we have to squint, at other times we need to stop speaking for a day. We have to close our eyes and listen to the world. If we don't change the angle of our vision, we won't see the whole show.

ART AND LIFE: A NECESSARY ISOMORPHISM

The art object made is not only a product of the moment or one of mere dexterity but a specific example of a general characteristic of its maker. When asked how long a particular work has taken, artists often quite accurately respond, "A lifetime." The things we make are signs of the things we are, seismographs of our internal state of affairs. If we recognize the parallelism between the structure and rhythm of our selves and the form and pattern of our images, we will be provided with a revealing display of our inner lives. As Joseph Zinker has pointed out,

> the creative process is therapeutic in itself because it allows us to express and examine the content and dimensions of our internal lives. We live full lives to the degree to which we find a full range of vehicles which concretize, symbolize, and otherwise give expression to our experiences.[18]

Thought of in this way, art can be said to be—and can be used as—the externalized map of our interior self. Scrutinizing this map merely for its surface aesthetic qualities is to miss the full content of art and thus to fail to employ the actual power of art to illuminate ourselves, even more, to transform ourselves to become the person we would prefer to be. Art is about art, and art is about describing the world. But above these functions, art is about exploring what it is to be human.

Drawing attention to this parallelism between the look of a work and the makeup of its author all too often invites the criticism of reducing art to psychotherapy. Once in the domain of therapy, art fails to attract aesthetic considerations. It is either art for art's own sake or art as a diagnostic instrument. This severing of the formal attributes of art from the psychological dimensions of art is similar to separating the qualities of mind from those of the body. You can do it, but by so doing you deprive one of its manifestation, and the other of its motivation.

Zinker also states that

> therapy is a process of changing awareness and behavior. The sine qua non of the creative process is change: the transformation of one form to another, of a symbol into an insight, of a gesture into a new set of behaviors, of a dream into a dramatic enactment. Thus creativity and psychotherapy are interconnected at a fundamental level: transformation, metamorphosis, change.[19]

Why not maintain the vital interdependency of creativity and therapy and focus on how each is portrayed in each? There can be no art that is not humanly authored, no human act that is not a product of a human mind. And in this same way there is no act that fails to reveal mind.

Every gesture and utterance emanates from within. By examining these external gestures and utterances we can infer what must lie below. This is the reason art has any poignancy at all. *On Not Being Able to Paint* by Joanna Field offers clear and dramatic descriptions of the author's employment of this isomorphism to extend the range and quality of her art while at the same time extending the quality of her personal life.

> Could one say that by finding a bit of the outside world, whether in chalk or paper, or in one's analyst, that was willing temporarily to fit in with one's dreams, a moment of illusion was made possible, a moment in which inner and outer seemed to coincide? Was it also true to say that it was by these moments that one was able to reestablish the bridge, mend the broken boat, and so be reawakened at least to the possibility of creative life in the real world? Was it not a legitimate hypothesis to suppose that by these moments of achieved fusion between inner and outer one was at least restored potentially to a life of action, a life in which one could seek to rebuild, restore, re-create what one loved, in actual achievement? . . . And this was made possible, both in a small way in free drawing, but more fully in psycho-analysis because in both the situation has well-defined limits, in neither is one committed to the repercussions that action in the real world brings. . . . I wanted to learn how to create, by painting, a true reciprocal relationship between dreams and what was outside; in fact to learn how to endow the objects of the external world with a spiritual life, 'action,' that was appropriate to their nature. . . . Both the gods and the demons were being brought down to earth, their power more ready to be harnessed to real problems of living, madness was becoming more domesticated and tamed to do real work in a real world. . . . So one came to know more clearly what one

loved and would want to cherish in living and what one hated and would seek to eliminate or destroy; and by this one's life developed a clearer pattern and coherence and shape and was less a blind drifting with the tides of circumstance.[20]

And here is Zinker's summary of this important link between creating art and creating a chosen life.

> Making art is a way of concretizing our need for a broader and deeper range of living. In the process of creating, we stretch our psyches, touching both personal and archetypal aspects of our origins.[21]

ART AND UNPREDICTABILITY

How safe and differently wonderful the world would be if we had the power to predict the future! To predict the future is to have unlimited power and access to untold fortune. It is a dream found in fable, myth, religion, and the talk of children. But (need one be told?) it is not the way the universe works. We know all too well that if we hold on to the notion that the universe unfolds in a smooth and determined fashion and hope that we will be able to predict the future, we will be crushed in our expectations, for the real world simply does not conform to this elusive hope. If we vest our energy in this fruitless direction, we must become exasperated as life continues to stream tantalizingly past us just beyond our grasp and our control. We must be able to live with what we all know to be the nature of the world; things change and they change in unpredictable ways. If we are to swim exuberantly in this sometimes turbulent stream, we must accommodate a substantial degree of anxiety in our lives. Rollo May says the following about anxiety:

> Creative people . . . are distinguished by the fact that they can live with anxiety, even though a high price may be paid in terms of insecurity, sensitivity, and defenselessness for the gift of the "divine madness."[22]

Starting off a creative process with the belief that we can predict and control the eventual outcome is, similarly, to squeeze out of the creative process its inherent evolutionary character and invite frustration. Not to allow the hand, eye, and spirit to learn from moment to moment throughout the creative process is to deny us access to an enormous quantity of new data that becomes uncovered, but is quickly covered over again by the veil of our own expectations. To constrain and deny what is natural and universal is to pit ourself against the universe. And guess what? We lose.

Earlier I stated that the more we see the more we know, the more we know, the more we see, and so on, endlessly. Placing this truism in the con-

text of the creative process, we may also say that if at the outset we already know what the outcome will look like, we deny a great deal of perceptual material that is bound to come our way. In the course of evoking the nascent image, the hand from time to time displays flourishes, makes marks, and chooses colors that are quite surprising in their novelty. Some of these displays are shocking, some contain ancient material dredged up from the past. Some of the images are too brazen, too nasty, too whatever for us to claim them as our own as of yet. Whatever the range of the new information, if we single-mindedly pursue the original image, we must blind ourselves to all this potential new richness, and in turn deny ourselves the consequential likelihood of personal and aesthetic growth.

We must disabuse ourselves of this flawed dream of predicting— and thus controlling—our world. We can't do it. Wishing to do so only frustrates us and inhibits our participation in life and art as it is. If we engage in the creative process as one who scoops up water believing they have captured the stream, we will end up making a piteously shallow imitation of a really grand thing, drained of its life force. If we are to be artists in and of life, we must plunge into the stream, allowing ourselves to feel the heave of its might. We can splash madly about, but in the end we must yield and permit it to buoy us up, touch us all over, filter through our hair, chill our bones, who knows, save our souls. This too is the stuff of art.

REPRESENTATION, ABSTRACTION: A FALSE DICHOTOMY

One final crippling concept of art that we will do well to set aside concerns the apparent irreconcilability of representation and abstraction. There seem to be two hostile camps in the field of art, one marching under the stripes of

Abstraction, the other rallying around the banner of Representation. I believe a false dichotomy is being made here, one that leads to mutual antagonism and a useless diversion of creative energy. So many neophyte artists torment themselves with this crisis of means—which they make into a crisis of identity—that I wish to offer a reframing and reconciliation.

Rather than slicing all of art into the two large, antagonistic categories of realism and abstraction, I would have you consider the view that *all* art is abstract as much as *all* art is representational. This is my brief: every made image involves an elaborate sequence of mental operations, from perception to selection through strategizing to representation. The meanest optical awareness no more resembles the mindlessness of the camera than the tropism of the amoeba resembles the spiritual yearnings of mankind (well, perhaps there may be a tiny resemblance . . .).

With close observation, we can identify several distinct and important mental operations in every act of portrayal, whether it is portrayed in its visual exactness or its symbolic equivalence. A survey of these mental operations at a rather gross level of behavior might include the following abbreviated sequence: (1) scanning the total region of attention, (2) selecting from the total field salient features, (3) elimination of material deemed peripheral or inconsequential, (4) setting of desired goals, (5) strategizing of means within the constraints and resources then available, (6) selection of appropriate materials and techniques in the pursuit of realistic goals, (7) effective employment of tools in the exercise of the plan, (8) evaluation of ends in terms of plan in terms of original goal, (9) termination of experience, and (10) reflection upon all of the above for subsequent similar endeavors. This series of sophisticated steps occurs each time we intend any act. Further, all these mental operations are exercised not once, but many times throughout the microseries of trials and errors and corrections that make up the simplest creative event, even painting a nice picture of a nice apple. This is an extremely complex *conceptual* process, culminating *not* in the creation of another "apple," but in a work of art, an externalized work of the mind. The painted apple now residing on the page may be banal and devoid of any deeper meaning than the fact that "this is a picture of a nice apple"; or it may be a sublime, Cézannesque apple, but in any case it is certainly not a real apple. It is a grand abstraction.

Representational art does not begin with the object; it begins with the fascination a human being feels upon witnessing a portion of the world. It is a fascination with the form, color, line, height, texture of the apple, not as apples grow, not as they taste, nor as they feel or smell, but from the single selected dimension of how they *look* from an aesthetic point of view. Other people are also interested in the look of apples—horticulturists, anthropologists, chefs, greengrocers, nutritionists—but only the artist is interested in the look of an apple from the specific perspective of the evocative expressiveness of its form. Is this not an abstraction, a mental event derived from a physical object? And in this way *all* art is in its essential nature and motive abstract, in that its goal is not to re-create the thing in the world, but to portray a mental event (fascination) derived from a mind's reaction to being witness to a segment of the world (in this case, that segment called Apple.)

All art is also always representational. The object of the mind's interest is not only objects, sunsets, apples, naked bodies; sometimes its interest turns to other items of attention, such as truth, beauty, meaning, value, hope, sadness, doubt, peace. Very real things that give people and civilizations their particular spin and texture. These very real "things" have no single physical embodiment; rather they impart to physical objects the qualities of meaning, value, utility, and feeling. Such elements manifest their presence on the physical plane by how they make physical things move and how they make people move intellectually and emotionally. Hence the representational objective of art is not to represent things; it is to represent what happens to humans when they confront things.

It is not quite accurate to say that the objective of art (be it portrayed figuratively or "abstractly") is to represent what happens to us as a consequence of encountering the world. A fuller description of the task would be to say our aim is to *discover* what happens to us as we consider things. This searching, active inquiry after what things *do* mean for us gives any work of art that deserves a second glance its fresh, just-discovered look. The work has that appearance because it appeared in that way; in other words, it was discovered, and what we see as we contemplate the artwork is the act of a person just uncovering something of great personal importance. What happens to us is not apples, what happens is feelings and thoughts as outcomes of observation—which are as real as apples: not as tasty, but delicious nonetheless.

Again, all art is representational in that it represents real things and real events, some of which exist in the physical dimension, while others exist in the dimension of thought. Whatever the plane of reality, all art derives from some dimension of reality. Some aspects of reality are not qualities found *in* things but *between* things. Interval speaks of relationships: intimacy, longing, waiting, frustration, consummation. Some qualities become apparant only when we examine the *sequence* of items, their direction, velocity, and the rhythm of the sequence. Other qualities of our world are to be discovered in noticing the rarity, the delicacy, the power of the thing to effect other things. Some dimensions of the reality we know are found in our *prior history* of associations with objects, which in turn trigger fields of emotions. All these things are real, all are important, and none are fixed in a specific form bound to a particular time and place. For those items that already exist

in the world, we have a ready vocabulary to work with. We mimic with the products of our hands what our eyes have observed and what our mind cherishes. We come upon a glistening bright red apple, it delights our senses, evokes fond memories, catches our fancy. We want to convey our excitement to others about "our" apple. True, it's a very complex, extremely intricate piece of thinking and coordination. But for most of us this is an everyday act of mind, and we do it so naturally and frequently that we rarely become aware that we are engaged in such a complex thought process.

As we have seen, not all awareness is taken up by fascination with the look of the physical dimension of the universe. Because these things (our feelings, our thoughts, our aspirations) have no preexistent presence in the world, we have to invent images in order to portray what is newly discovered. Of course the image may look strange and appear to be abstract. Anything come upon for the very first time looks abstract because it has no frame of reference to be named or placed within a context of prevailing reality. But it's not *abstract* so much as it is *original.* For the infant the whole world is abstract until the shapes, movements, textures, patterns, noises of the world are given names, uses, and value. Then that red and green, shiny, smooth, roundish thing about the size of my hand becomes an Apple. And Abstraction becomes Representation.

The same with verbal language. To the nonspeaker all language is an abstraction of noise with a fascinating gurgle of pops, clicks, wooshes, and silences sewn together with a special range of pitch and rhythm. If we stay with it for a while, and are helped along by a guide who is a veteran maker of that "noise," we eventually pick apart the items in the stream, notice their particular contours, and assign specific meanings to each pop and gurgle. At this point we shift our focus from the "abstract" qualities of the rhythm, textures, pitch, pacing, variety of sounds of the noise, and settle down to paying attention to the meanings carried along by the code that relates sound to meanings. In this way, the new becomes familiar, abstraction gives way to representation.

Abstract art, then, can be said to be the representation in palpable form of ideas or feelings that themselves are not necessarily abstract but *immaterial*. And isn't that what all art does, after all—create things on the physical plane from things on the planes of consciousness?

Many artists, novices and veterans alike, expend their creative energies battling the claims of these two apparently divergent camps. It is a waste of our brief moment in the light to be hemmed in between the conventions of abstraction and those of representation and to believe that we must choose one or the other for our mode of expression. Critics have repeatedly taken it upon themselves to declare the poverty of one and the timeliness of or necessity for the other. They urge us to respect the picture plane or to violate the picture plane; they proclaim figuration is dead, or that figuration lives on; they demand that no sentiment be allowed, or that feeling be all; they say we must not lie, or that all there are are lies. Not that these issues don't matter; but they are only temporal, local opinions. As soon as we perceive a shifting of context—as all context must shift—we gladly throw them over to tearfully embrace the next set of opinions.

We can wrestle with more worthwhile things than this. Why not acknowledge that all representation is an act of abstraction and that all abstraction must be conveyed through the act of representation and be done with it? And let us now get on with what we are ultimately about, seeking the light, seeking greater clarity, expanding our consciousness, and constantly increasing the vocabulary whereby we discover and declare our presence in the world. If we must wrestle with something, why not struggle against staying in the shallows and grapple our way toward the profundity of the depths? Abstraction *and* representation, beauty *and* meaning.

2

Advice to the Journeyman

NO MORE SECONDHAND ART

Imagine how it might feel to be the first human who, absently scratching a finger through the earth, sees an image of something appear, some vague but recognizable creature. This clay thing looks like that "real" thing. Here, right in your hands is a thing somehow like the live thing. And your hands scratching in this dirt made it, created it, gave birth to it. With eyes that can take in only so much, and with a mind at the dawn of its development, you stare at this—what? What do you see? What is this thing you have just made? What powers does it possess? What did you just do? Can you make another thing like that again? Are you the parent of the thing? What just happened to you, to the thing, to the world?

A creature appeared, silent, unmoving, but a creature did appear when you scratched the earth with your fingers. You try it again: nothing, just scratchings. Try it again: nothing. Try it again: nothing again. Again. Again. Wait: something, something. It happened again, a thing is here, you scratched the earth and a thing appeared from the earth. Not the same thing as before, a new thing, you again created something that was more than nothing, and somewhat less than living. Touch it: nothing. Speak to it: nothing. Scratch it more and more: it is gone, back into the earth. It appears when you scratch the earth, but only sometimes. And it hides, goes into the earth when you scratch it more. This thing. This power you sometimes have. You do not know it yet, you may never know it, but you will never be the same, and the world will never be the same for you again. You, the creator and destroyer of things.

With your hands you can bring things into the world. Animal-things, people-things, god-things, thought and feeling things. You birthed the thing, but how, from where? Perhaps these things came to you as powers loaned from the gods. Perhaps the earth itself, when you scratch it in certain ways, gives you these things. Why have these things been given to you and not to others? Now you can do things that no one else can do, and there is a separation between you and the others. What is happening?

Before, there were two worlds. The world of everthing "out there," and the "you" that saw that world through the windows of your eyes. Now there are three worlds. The world out there, the world "in here," and the world of things you make. Made by only one parent. Appearing alive, but not alive. The gods speak to you in dreams by putting images in your head. Have the gods spoken to you again? Are these things you made really god-things, and are you the midwife, the vessel?

What else can be made? Such power in your hands! You take clay up in your hands and squeeze it, and from its formlessness you pull limbs, heads, torsos. With your fingers you press in eye holes, mouth holes. You make him virile, you make her fruitful. You make them run, you make them die, you make them live again. Who are you that you can do such things? Are these not the doings of gods, the stuff of gods? Have you crossed the sacred line separating men from gods? Will the gods notice and demand retribution, homage? Perhaps you can give these things, the best of these things, to them as a sign that the differences between humans and gods is still firm and in place.

Will they be pleased about your precociousness, forgive your transgression, honor your accomplishment? Will they in their jealousy and omnipotence crush you along with all the little things you have made that steal from them their rightful powers? The world no longer fits together in the same way, now that you share with the gods the power to create and destroy.

The experiences of the first person who ever drew recur each time any one of us in our naiveté rubs our hands across the world and leaves our own special mark. We can experience anew the wonder of being the first person who ever drew out of the earth, from nothing, some thing that is somehow alive and real. We can experience again that power, that sense of being deeply connected to and with the world. The ability to fashion a world, even if it be a tiny world, as we see fit is to partake in the exhilaration of the gods.

UNCOVERING THE ORIGINAL ME

To create art drawn from within is to create a world of our own and also to uncover an all-but-forgotten original, primal self. Sometimes life's circumstances bring back vivid memories of when we were quite young, when everything was new, when myth, fairy tale, and worldly events were interwoven into the seamless fabric of our life. In the seriousness of our adulthood we believe this early self has become lost to us and is irretrievably gone. This original self was insatiably curious, excited about all the astonishing things and events of this world, sensuously embedded in the world and tickled pink about it. Its waking and sleeping life was full of adventurous experiments and confrontations with unknown territory. It wept freely, laughed openly, and felt itself grow daily physically, intellectually, socially, and spiritually. This lost self came fully loaded with exquisite equipment. Now that earlier edition of our self seems gone, and its exquisite equipment somehow now rusted shut from neglect.

Interestingly, this original self seems also to have been rather artistic; it loved to make things, intricate, finely made things, privately meaningful things. There seemed to be an easy and graceful way of playing, fantasizing, creating stories and things, sometimes with others, often alone.

When we do occasionally contrive our lives so as to uncover (however fleetingly) our original self, it is clear that we are releasing something already there rather than creating it. There is an immediate sense of recognition, often accompanied by sorrow, later to be followed by quiet but deep joy. Finally, a new sense of self-confidence and heightened vitality ensues, a calm and enduring sense of personal power succeeds the initial reactions to this recovery.

The sorrow seems to be due to having been so close to this precious self and ignoring it for so long. Sorrow, too, at what all too often has been allowed to replace this wondrous self: flat years of denial, grim rounds of carrying out duties, doing the appropriate thing at the right time. Sorrow, perhaps, for the years spent in denying this original self the light of day and the privilege of being alive.

Yet sadness or remorse is invariably followed by the joy of reconciling the responsible and cultured adult self with the recently uncovered spontaneous and perpetually naive self. There is a sense of coming home, of finally feeling at home and whole in the world, and the rejoining of the two selves is accompanied by an increase of energy and a certain calmness in the certitude of personal well-being. There seems to be a greater appetite for life and for exploring the further reaches of the physical, intellectual, emotional, and spiritual domains.

The making of art can be an instrument by which we may reacquaint our current self with our original self. We can shape the making of art so as to help us realize that our original self is still alive and recoverable. Once reacquainted, we are likely to find a wise, powerful, and remarkably witty companion has been restored to us, to accompany us through life. The creative process engenders other supportive qualities of mind as well: these are discussed in the following section.

NO ONE KNOWS BETTER THAN YOU

One of the very few things I did learn in school was that I was not the best at anything. No matter how hard I racked my brains, prepared for tests, or shaded in that drawing of a crumpled paper bag, there was always some kid who did it better. If I did manage to get the best mark in my class, I certainly never made it past those quarter finals to the big leagues of best in the grade, not to mention best in the school, best in the district (city, state, region, division, nation, world). Some smart, fast, talented kid was always in front of me, way in front. That gets to you after a while. For some, never being first may have the dubious benefit of cultivating a healthy degree of humility, but for me—and I don't believe I am alone (there were plenty of kids in back of *me*)—the uninterrupted experience of being bested diminished my sense of self-worth and self-confidence.

Since the other kids in the class were so smart and I was not, it became obvious to me that "they" knew something that I didn't, something "out there." Clearly I was deficient, empty of correct (or even much) information, and if I wanted to succeed in life, or at least get through school, I had better know a great deal more about the world than I did. I therefore set about to know. Turning what meager gifts I was given to the task, I went to the library, walked up to the "A" section, took out the very first book, and launched into the world, starting with that portion inhabited by aardvarks. Some short time later, I pulled ashore at acoela, which you may remember are a group of worms belonging to the Turbellaria family and having no digestive tract. No sooner had I begun my rather simple linear conquest of the knowable world than my plan revealed its inadequacy. The world "out there" was growing bigger and I was growing smaller, quite the opposite of what I had in mind. My confidence in my intellect had taken a turn for the worse, if that was possible. This remained the case until I came upon another class of questions: questions that did not have their answers in the world "out there," but "in here," in personal history, in imagination and dreaming, in assertions of will, value, and belief. This other class of questions did not become apparent to me in one incident but over a course of time in which I saw and read much and during long reflective sessions in my studio, alone and with other artists, particularly with my colleague Seymour Segal. In this domain there were no other contenders. There was no repository of truth or data outside my own mindfulness. I became the subject, object, and instrument of my attempts at mentation. I did better in this domain. Most everyone does.

This noncompetitive knowing is a special reward of creative enterprises. It is quite delicious to carry on an investigation, personally arrive at a response, and not feel compelled to measure the worth of your findings against those of others. Others no longer pose a potential threat to your own degree and kind of intelligence. Their responses are valuable just as a journey to a distant land is valuable, not for the sake of comparing the quality of your life with theirs, but for the sake of witnessing the world and thus deepening the quality of your life experience.

To "draw from within" is to draw upon a source of wisdom that no one else could possibly have; it is a step that places you in a quiet and exclusive domain. Here, there is no one else to turn to. No one, however loving or intelligent, can accompany you on this inward journey. And the very solitariness of the quest brings about a sense of your own self-sufficiency.

As true as it is that we live within a community of others, it is equally true we are born and die alone. There are essential privacies that we are destined to maintain. These deep troughs of uniqueness are our particular gift and genius. So much of our life is standard, requiring conventional thoughts and behavior, that we forget that each of us is one of a kind, one whose life will either manifest our unique display of intelligence and enrich the story of humankind or fail to embroider the fabric of being human.

Creative engagements wake us up to the task of contributing to human history by accepting the challenge to compose our own story—a challenge that, if unaccepted, remains without takers.

Questions designed to provoke answers that can be measured against a norm and against each other make life competitive. We often use the answers to these kinds of questions not for their own worth, but as instruments with which we measure our status relative to others. There is really little intrinsic value in knowing the dates of inauguration of all the presidents of the United States, but if you are the only one in the class to do so, you are the smartest kid in the class, which is certainly of value in the world of status seekers.

Creative responses are those which have no comparative worth. They are of utility only to the person who responds to them. These responses may themselves be questions: "Why *did* I say that? What *does* that form, that gesture, those colors, that silence mean? Why do I feel a need for the presence of that blue, when it seems not to fit the rest of the image?" As a consequence of being touched in such a way as to uncover and awaken the person who, at root, we are, the unique potentiality that we are becomes manifest in the world, to us. The mere fact that we have been given life doesn't mean that we realize the nature of the life we are given. The creative process has the potential to wake us up to the vast unexplored domain of our own nature. No one has been there before, no one can enter it except us. No one can challenge our story. We are the only ones who can explore this

46

territory and return to tell the news. The encounters remind us of this by indicating points of access, doorways to our natural domain, and by carefully designing encounters, we can provide ourselves with handles to doors.

SELF-FULL, NOT SELFISH

If we cannot be alone, if we take being alone as being lonely, we will infrequently (or only partially) allow ourselves past the threshold of the ordinary and into the arena of the creative process. For to be at the very center of the creative act means to stand quite alone, without external companions with whom to share the burden of bringing something forth from apparent nothingness. There are essential moments when we must be *without* allies to point out the way, to reassure our faltering steps, to set limits, or to affirm hesitant beginnings. At the center of the creative act is our solitary self, away from the world as it is, facing the world as it becomes, as it emerges from our fingertips.

We often feel we must be in relationship with someone in order to experience the sensation of our own vividness. We feel that when we are alone we are cut off from a vital source for the definition of who we are and what we are. Without immediate companionship we often feel bereft of purpose, identity, and vitality. Unless we are actively nurturing someone else, or in turn being nurtured, we feel unloved and unloving. Alone, we long for the company of others, feel naked, invisible, meaningless. And as long as we feel that we are inadequate, insufficient, we will rely on others to provide orientation, definition, and purpose for our life. While we are at it, we might as well ask them to also paint our pictures and sing our songs. And of course, many of us do.

This is not to say that in order to make art one must live out one's life in solitude. Dialogue, companionship, and communion are essential qualities of the human condition. But there are periods of the creative process when one must stand alone. This does *not* mean standing without resources or standing lonely in the world, for we are inextricably embedded in the companionship of sunshine, moonlight, and landscape, and the world is not dumb or dead. We come marvelously equipped into a world offering a cornucopia of things to see, touch, smell, taste, and hear, and we come with wiring to dream, remember, imagine. We do enter and exit this world one by one, and we may very well be solitary, but we certainly are not without companionship or resources.

Why couldn't *we* be our own dearest friend or at least *one* of our dearest friends? Why couldn't we take for one of our life's works the exploration of the reaches of our own imagination? Why not trust ourselves to always be there for us, never to abandon us, to be lenient, forgiving, loving, and respectful? And most importantly, can we not be a source of strength, wisdom, and entertainment for ourselves? Why expect to receive from others what we don't ask of ourselves? The experience of drawing from within helps us to uncover such a companion. This companion already resides within our outer form, but its contours are all too often blurred. Only as we take the effort to seek and define them are its qualities revealed. The deeper we go into the quiet recesses of our mind the deeper and more substantial this self appears.

As we permit ourselves to go into regions of thought we have forbidden ourselves, we will find quietly waiting there our original self. The more playful and joyful we permit ourself to be, the more exuberant our original self will be as our companion. In our solitary dreams and wanderings, griefs and ecstasies, if we seek inward and allow our original self to be present, being alone will lose its sting. In alliance with our wondrous, spontaneous, and original self, our cultivated, deliberate self will do splendid business with the world of things and of the mind and of the heart.

This is the goal of drawing from within, the potential power of real art making. Image making has these capabilities because every stroke we make, every color we choose and do not choose, corresponds to a personal quality within. As we draw from within, as we do regularly when we dream, so do we uncover and discover the within of ourselves. Finding and mapping and extending our sense of self wakes us up not only to what is, but to what might be.

DREAMS: OUR FIRST AND NATIVE LANGUAGE

Think of a vivid dream you once had. Recollect that dream and for a moment allow it to pass before your eyes again, the people, the events, the place, the drama of it. Did you notice anything "wrong" with those images? Were they poorly made? Were they less expressive or intense than you needed them to be? Did you hesitate to play out the scene while you worked on getting the features of the faces just right or as you tried to get the correct perspective in the buildings, rooms, street, and cars? Did you have any trouble drawing the animation of the figures? Was it difficult to image them running, sitting, coming forward, or receding? Isn't it remarkable what an incredibly adept, confident, and expressive artist you are in the creation of your dreams? How is it that no horse, house, person, or event is too difficult to "dream-draw"? You just image what needs imaging and do it so powerfully and convincingly that even you, the artist, are caught up in the drama of the dream.

No one has to be taught how to dream. No one has to be taught how to dream in perspective or how to image people, places, or things in dreams. In dreams we are never self-conscious about how poorly crafted our images are. People of every race, every age, every class, every intellect dream, and no one complains about the artistic quality of his or her dream images. Even dogs dream, in dog-made images.

Dreams, the images we create in our mind's eye, are always pertinent, expressive, compelling and convincing, mystifying and edifying. They are never shallow, never gratuitous, never decorative. Every single one of us is a craftsman of dreams; our dream images are always perfect and evocative. Visual thinking and visual imagery is our *native language*. If we can get out from under our commonly held beliefs about art and art training, we can create conscious images that are as easy, as compelling, and as significant as our dreams.

What has been told to us about the making of "waking drawing" which so hobbles our hand and our waking mind? What have we done to ourselves to mask the ability we all have in the making of dreams, so that our waking images are impoverished? What we have told ourselves and allowed ourselves to believe about how art is produced has twisted and frustrated our native abilities to creative powerful, articulate images.

The enterprise of creating personal imagery is defeated before the brush is ever picked up because of the wrongheaded common notion of how images emerge, how they serve, and how they may be "taught." We need to sweep away the disabling myths and practices and goals of art teaching and allow the natural inborn artist that each one of us inherently is to reveal itself.

A MAP IS NOT A JOURNEY

One concept that interferes with the play of the imagination and the open search for meaning is the misconception that life in time is somehow analogous to a map of a portion of space. Maps are extremely powerful instruments for orientation, direction, and prediction; however, they are not identical to the reality to which they refer, and if taken as such they work against exploration, wonder, and discovery. If we liken engaging in a creative endeavor to taking a journey with the help of a map, several important inhibitions of the creative endeavor and journeying are revealed.

A map offers fixed points on a circumscribed portion of the surface of the world. These points are all in exact and consistent relation to one another. Out of the vast number of items actually contained in that territory, only the locations of an extremely few select items from a few categories of items are displayed. A legend decodes the symbols used; the scale of the map to the actual territory and the absolute and relative location of due north are also provided. That's a map.

We use maps so frequently to get from one place to another in space that we tend to carry over that predilection when we try to go from one place to another in the course of a creative endeavor. And then serious problems arise. Our fear of running off the map, wandering off into the unknown and getting lost in physical territory is transposed in creative enterprises to concern about running out of imagination, running out of patience, or running out of courage. As a consequence we not only stay within the boundaries of the canvas, but we stay within the boundaries of taste, boundaries of size, complexity, ambition, fullness of expression, and so on.

We fear getting lost. We believe that we are not lost when we know where something else is and how far we are from it. Note that in order for us to know where *we* are, we have always to be conscious of where something *else* is. Not knowing the nature and whereabouts of other things causes us to feel empty, disoriented, frightened, and vulnerable. In order to overcome this disabling state of mind, we seek familiar things. We scan the surrounding environment, passing quickly from thing to thing until we alight on something familiar. And as soon as we do we believe we are found. We know where we are, we are safe.

The disabling effect of this thought process on our creative endeavors is this: if we feel lost without the familiar, without guidelines, without interior orientation, we will never stray far from home. We will stay around familiar territory, which is nice, but certainly not news. Pleasant, but certainly not an adventure. Pretty, but not bold.

As we move across that canvas, or (in terms of other art forms) that stage, that silence before the empty page, there will be periods when we do not know where we are going. Throughout the creative enterprise there will be periods in which we *cannot* know where we are going, simply because the whole purpose of the enterprise is to chart new courses, to land up who-knows-where but at least not back home. The ability to carry on in these circumstances derives in no small measure from having a distinct sense of personal orientation, a self that knows its own center and is unafraid of being who it is. In this way, although we may not know where we are relative to external signs we are never quite lost and—to be honest—never quite found.

During the creative process, rather than orient ourselves as we do on a map, concerning ourselves with how close or far we are from "home," we may consider orienting ourselves on an alternative scale, one of depth or degree. In this way, questions such as "How far away am I from home?" are replaced with questions such as "How deep am I? How far from the surface of things? How high am I? How far have I allowed my imagination to soar? How stiff am I? How much sweep and scope have I permitted myself? How available am I to what I see, remember, imagine?" With these types of questions in mind the journey into uncharted territories takes on a cast of exhilaration and increasing profundity. We may not know where we are going, but we will be gaining a greater sense of where we are and a deeper appreciation of *who* we are.

Continuing to employ the metaphor of mapping we might describe the creative encounter as being one in which we are at a perpetual crossroads. At every moment we are free to make—we must make—decisions that may send us off in some new direction: With each stroke of the brush, we must ask ourselves: "Shall I stay where I am, or shall I retreat to some safer, more familiar ground? Shall I push on down that well-trodden road? Shall I take this narrow trail? Shall I cut my own trail?" Every stroke, every reach for a color, every silence and pause offers us this display of choices. If we do use the map of depth rather than the conventional map of length and seek within for our orientation rather than without, we shift our focus away from questions such as "Am I lost? How can I get home? Will someone rescue me?" to more self-reliant, adventurous questions: "How deep, how honest, how full are these steps I've just taken? Where do I go from here?"

SEE FOR YOURSELF

Another way to approach the problem of fresh seeing may be explored as follows.

Secondhand accounts of the world surround us; we live through hearsay. This is not a problem in itself, but it does become a serious one if we fail to recognize the difference between vicarious experience and direct witnessing. To illustrate this point, take any news report in the daily paper or on television. As everyone knows, what gets seen by the reporter is not what gets said by the reporter, and this in turn is not identical with what eventually appears in the media. The reporter's subjective statements become the primary source with which others now have a creative experience. The editor, the publisher, the copy editor, the screenwriter, the cameraman, the director, the producer, all have a go with the material passed down to them, each one seeing it uniquely and uniquely reshaping it before passing it on eventually (and much altered) to us.

Finally we "see" a television special on Faulkner's South, or Van Gogh, or the Renaissance, and we feel we are now in the know. We know about Van Gogh. Even more, we feel we have come to know Van Gogh himself. And we speak authoritatively about the torment of Van Gogh; we even take on some of his painting style. (Forgetting that his painting style was also his emotional style—want that too?) We paint things about sunsets over the hills of Provence, and the glowing wheat fields of the Midi. In our romantic enthusiasm we allow ourselves to forget that what we know of Van Gogh is but a shadow on the wall, a chimera.

We have the responsibility to see for ourselves and not settle for hearsay. If we live our lives in rumor and hearsay, who we are and what we do will reflect not the world of our own experience but the diluted, inaccurate reflections cast by others.

Seeing something firsthand is to meet the thing. To confront something one-to-one is to be taken up and changed by that thing and to change the thing as a consequence of our reactions to it. Seeing the thing directly is having an experience with all the complexity of thought and feelings and somatic reactions that accompany all experiences. To hold a beloved person in our arms, to feel her warmth, her hair against our face, breathe in her aroma and hear the rhythm of her breathing is to have an utterly different experience than reading in *People* magazine about Charles and Di doing similar things.

When so much of the world comes to us through the media, we slowly, imperceptibly come to believe that we are still living in the world of people, places, things, and events when in sad fact we are living in the world of newspapers, words, pictures, electronic blips of light and sound. Like the denizens of the cave described in Plato's *Republic,* we too have taken the shadows cast on the wall for the actual objects. We talk to and about shadows while the actual world glides unobtrusively by. Imagery generated from experiences that refer to the world but are not themselves the stuff referred to can hardly be compelling.

Since seeing is not a simple matter of optics but a complex series of events gathering to it our collective personal histories, our momentary state of mind and body, it is fair to say what we "see" is a compound image consisting of what is "out there" and who is "in here." What we see is who we are, overlayered with whatever is there to be seen. Therefore no two people ever "see" the same thing. No two versions of reality are identical. We all know this, but when push comes to shove we conveniently forget it.

In order to become intelligible, seeing requires describing. How a person describes the world is always a personally edited version of what has been "seen." How our mind organizes sense data into coherent, purposeful concepts determines what get said. Each of us uniquely forms meaning from our personally selected data bank. This unique cast of our minds is in fact what makes us *us.* So what gets said is different from what gets seen, and what gets seen is different from what is seeable.

In *I and Thou,* Martin Buber speaks of the uncompromising integrity necessary for this encounter between the real self and the real thing "out there."

> The act includes a sacrifice and a risk. This is the sacrifice; the endless possibility that is offered up on the altar of the form. . . . This is the risk: the primary word can only be spoken with the whole being. He who gives himself to it may withhold nothing of himself. The work does not suffer me, as do the tree and the man, to turn aside and relax in the world of *It;* but it commands. If I do not serve it aright it is broken, or it breaks me.
>
> I can neither experience nor describe the form which meets me, but only body it forth. And yet I behold it, splendid in the radiance of what confronts me. . . . I do not behold it as a thing among the "inner" things nor as an image of my "fancy," but as that which exists in the present. . . .
>
> To produce is to draw forth, to invent is to find, to shape is to discover. In bodying forth I disclose. . . . The work produced is a thing among things, able to be experienced and described as a sum of qualities. But from time to time it can face the receptive beholder in its whole embodied form.[23]

How can we come before life with no intermediaries and bear witness to our own experiences? It is not easy, it is even difficult, but it can be done, and it is necessary. We can draw upon what we have personally witnessed. We can tell our own story if we can be candid, simple, and unflinching. This *is* the ground of art. Again, Buber:

> All real living is meeting.
>
> The relation to the *Thou* is direct. No system of ideas, no foreknowledge, and no fancy intervene between *I* and *Thou.* The memory itself is transformed, as it plunges out of its isolation in to the unity of the whole. No aim, no lust, and no anticipation intervene between *I* and *Thou.*[24]

The challenge is to see directly, freshly. Not through inherited eyes, but through original eyes, for the first time. The challenge of art is the same challenge that life presents us with moment by moment: Can we awaken from our casual viewing of a stupendous world? Can we free up some of our mind from memory and give some over to perception and some to imagination and be present and available to life as it streams over us? Can we meet life raw, accept its impact and later convey that experience to others in some full utterance or gesture?

No one can stand between us and the blazing universe. Neither the wisest nor the best must stand between us and our direct touching of the world. Others may position us, bring us to ripeness, but then we must take leave of them, set out on our journey and step forward into life on our own. With all respect and appreciation for what has been given to us, we must see for the first time this soul-smacking, heart-rending gift of—world.

AM I GOOD ENOUGH?

A journey of any magnitude is bound to raise some stock-taking before the moment of embarkation. As a consequence, there are several questions that we often ask ourselves whenever we set out on any journey into uncharted domains. These types of questions are the same ones neophyte art students and even certain more experienced artists ask themselves whenever they engage in the creative process and in so doing stand in their own way: Am I skilled enough? Am I smart enough? Am I talented enough? Am I sensitive enough? Am I . . . enough?

These questions are always lethal when asked at the outset of a creative engagement because there are always two answers to each question, both of which are always true, always opposed to each other, and always wrong. The first answer to any of the questions is: No! We are never skilled, smart, or talented enough, because there is *always* more we can be, and if we were smarter we would do different and probably better things. Compared to what can be known and is known, we know less. Compared with at least someone else on the planet, we most likely are not the smartest. It's sad, but it's true.

Quite opposed to this first answer is the equally true response: Yes! We *are* smart enough, simply because at any point in time we can only be exactly who we are and what we are. We will only and *always* be what we are at that moment. If we were smarter, we would be smarter, but still exactly who we are, doing exactly what we are doing, wanting to be smarter. That will be true until our dying day and then some. While we wait because something is lacking in our makeup, life is inexorably going on. Our visitation privileges are running out. So, we might as well start getting down to work because, like it or not, our time is running out.

However we respond to the question, "Am I ——— enough?", be it yes or no, the answer will always be destructive. We can never win the encounter with such a question, because the very underlying assumption of "Am I ——— enough?" is a faulty appraisal of the human condition and a false understanding of what it does take to engage in creative enterprises.

This false assumption is that we *must* be or have enough of something in order to successfully engage in creative activities. But just what are these somethings? What do they look like? How many of them are necessary? And who determines what and how much is necessary for us to join the fracas? Any doubts we may have concerning our personal imperfections will therefore be magnified by a confrontation with such unknowables.

The other reason why the question "Am I —— enough?" is bound to be lethal is that the question forces us to compare ourselves to some external standard. Since standards are always hypothetical extremes and people are not, real people will always, *must* always fall short of the standard. We are all imperfect versions of some external standard, some Platonic absolute. We are supposed to lose. So don't do it. Do not engage this tar baby.

There are other, more propitious mind-sets with which we may approach the creative process. Rather than paralyzing ourselves with the existential bone-crusher "Am I good enough?" we would do better to ask ourselves questions that invoke no comparisons. Instead, we could become interested in *describing* the new terrain being uncovered or invented.

In this frame of mind we would be curious about how honest, candid, and accurate we are in our portrayals of the urgencies of our inner life. What does happen when we allow our hand to have its sway, as lightly reined in by the scrutiny of the conscious mind as we dare? Rather than rushing to obliterate "mistakes," we might become interested in just what our "mistakes" actually look like. We might study these unpreferred marks and try to appreciate what about them we do not identify with or why they do repel us. Why are we made uncomfortable with the products of our own mind and hand? What powers do these marks contain that we will not or cannot use?

We might also ask ourselves how far we dare travel before feeling lost, or out of control, or past our boundaries of propriety. We might do well to test the firmness of these boundaries within which we feel comfortable, sane, whole, and see if they are not as rigid as we take them to be. We might ask ourselves what it looks like on the other side of the boundary, what it feels like to trespass into (self-) forbidden pastures and thickets. In other words, instead of "Am I good enough, am I ready enough?" we might ask ourselves what would it feel like, how would we proceed if we *did* feel good enough and did feel ready to dance with the universe?

BEYOND RIGHT AND WRONG

Just as preoccupation with whether or not we are sufficiently prepared for creative enterprises inevitably creates profound barriers to creative enterprises, so does anxiety about being right or being wrong. If we value the notion of right and wrong relative to creative endeavors, we cloak ourselves with a weighty garment that is bound to inhibit spontaneous movement. Can we have a dream that is wrong? Can we have a right dream? But that is too passive a way to describe dreaming. Can we *make* a wrong or right dream? I don't think so. Evaluating a dream along a right/wrong continuum is to examine the worth of dreams with a wholly useless instrument. We *can* make shallow or profound dreams. We may examine a dream with intensity and integrity, or we may choose to ignore it and let it pass us by. Each confrontation with the dream brings its own reward.

As with dreams, so it is with any other deliberate act of creativity. Rather than employ the criteria of right and wrong with which to judge creative endeavors we might substitute other, more fitting and more illuminating criteria. Instead of asking, "Is it right?" (or really, "Am I right?" or "Am I wrong?"), we could ask, "How honest was I in disclosing what I know and feel? How deep did I allow myself to go? What range of new territory have I explored? How close to the center of my sense of self did I dare to go? What really resonates within me as true in the work, what is false, tinny?"

The notion that there *is* a right and a wrong in creative expression is inherently debilitating. Invariably what is "right" or "wrong" is defined by current and local taste and comes to us from the outside. "Right" and "wrong" always pits "us" against "them," and more often than not we lose. It is we who are found wanting. Extrinsic systems of evaluations always create winners and losers and always require us to look outside ourselves to know who we are and how we are doing. This lack of inner determinants makes the would-be creator beholden to foreign standards and directions.

We cannot act with integrity or be spontaneous and original when we place between ourselves and our canvas the conclusions and values of others. Right and wrong are always associated with good and bad. Good and bad always have ethical connotations; hence in judging our work (and worth) using right and wrong as our scale, we not only often come out inept, we also feel ethically deficient. Given such heavy odds that one will be judged inept and ethically unsound, is it any wonder that so few engage in creative encounters of any depth and risk?

There are two critical phases of the creative enterprise in which we would do well to avoid judgment: in the initial phase of the work, and again later, when the process has run its course and there is a substantially formed product to consider. To avoid the pitfalls of good and bad as determinants, we could begin the initial phase with the open-ended statement "Let's see what happens." This necessarily naive proposal opens our enterprise to experimentation, to a setting aside of preconceptions, specific expectations, and foreseeable conclusions. There are no hypotheses to prove or disprove, no image in mind and no standards of worth with which to judge the value of the act and its object. At the outset, our goal might simply be to do things we never did before. Later, toward completion, our goal would be to carefully and fully describe what had occurred. Having created things never made before (at least by us) as a consequence of this open-ended experimentation, we will do well to slow down and carefully, thoroughly, scrutinize and describe exactly what has occurred. Shifting one's focus from judgment to description may sound like an easy and rather innocuous exercise. It is neither. It is in fact an extremely powerful intellectual process offering feedback that can reveal subtle qualities of the enterprise, qualities that otherwise remain obscure, and vital information with which to guide subsequent work.

The thing just made is really new; it has never been seen before by anyone, including its author. The important thing—the *only* thing—to do now is to become acquainted with it. This takes more time than one usually anticipates, much more than one usually gives. The purpose of such looking is not to see how to improve it. This "seeing" of the piece is like the careful seeing given to an infant or a loved one. Every wrinkle is caressed, every tone and shade is seen, now with one eye, now the other. Tiny details are explored, larger patterns of several elements are noticed and run across over and over again.

What is the worth of this nonjudgmental seeing? What good can come from this elaborate expenditure of active seeing time? There are several rewards. One is this: just because we made the image doesn't mean we see it in all of its complexity of meanings. Material comes forward from the conscious mind, but material also seeps up from the subconscious and the collective unconscious, often expressing itself in the seeming accidents of our particular gestures. The marks the hand brings forward can lie there completely unobserved and therefore remain undiscovered. We may be in new territory, but it can have no effect unless we are *aware* of the fact and take pains to map the details and the large patterns of this new domain.

The other value of practicing nonjudgmental looking is that the longer we look the more we see. The more we see, the more there is to consider, to weave into new concepts and values. To see new things in a created piece is to see new aspects of ourself. The piece becomes more dense with meanings and richer in evidence the more we take cognizance of it. Too often we see our work as shallow, and all too often this is because we view our own work too quickly, too casually. What we take for an empty canvas may be only a weak moment of seeing. As in all our activities, the more we see the better we see, and vice versa.

Twenty minutes spent drawing between other obligations will yield images that look like they were made in twenty minutes between other obligations. If we would honor the creative dimension of ourselves we must give ourselves an appropriate amount of time to do so. There does not seem to be a set figure for how much time is needed to fully employ imagination: each person requires different units of time to work creatively. What is clear is the necessity to discover which units are most advantageous for us and to somehow insist upon that for ourselves.

In addition, we need a buffer period between the chaos of the day and our creative periods if the latter are to have a character distinct from the former. The conscious, in-the-world mind needs time to slow down and cease its constant harangue of duty, responsibility, tidiness, and propriety. To become aware of the subtle, creative mind—the mind that is in touch with visions, imagination, and memories—the conscious mind that normally dominates and masks it must be silenced. Then images and their accompanying feelings drawn from deep within emerge, at first unfocused, a bit thin and wobbly. They will become more vivid only if allowed the time to do so. Most of us offer our image-making mind insufficient time to generate altered states of consciousness with their attendant images and visions, and then come to believe we are deficient of imagination or have weak and infrequent creative impulses. As a consequence, we abandon the creative enterprise altogether. The actual difficulty often is much less intractable (if no less debilitating): it may simply be that we have left our imagination in the developing solution for too short a time. No wonder we come up with blank or weak impressions!

Some people can shift focus from one mind to the other in a few minutes; others need thirty minutes. One is not better or more creative than another; each is just different. Each of us must experiment and find the correct developing time for ourselves—not once and for all, but periodically, for that time will probably change as our lives evolve. We need to keep adjusting our time frame to accommodate our creative needs and enterprises.

Most ordinary chores of our daily lives require quick perception and tough, reality-based decision making. Opportunities flash by in conversations on the streets, in stores, business places, and homes. The infinite domestic tasks that arise are no-nonsense, matter-of-fact situations demanding no-nonsense responses. Yet if we carry the same mental disposition into the arena of creative endeavors we will fail to notice the tracings of thought that are slow in unfolding, light in presence, and intricate in pattern. If we wish to attend to other dimensions of reality, it is necessary to first put aside the perceptual and intellectual equipment we use to catch ordinary reality and instead try slow seeing, elongated gestures, light and quiet thoughts and gestures. For a while, as we stand in front of our media, we can let things slide, let things pass, let things be. There will be other times for culling out the flax from the dross. But not now. Let us go lightly at first; the heavy hand of judgment will assert itself soon enough.

A keen eye is essential for steering a preferred course, but if it is exercised prematurely, we will never travel to lands other than the ones we already have been to. In fact, we can employ both judgment and imaginative play if we separate the phases and the pacing of the creative enterprise: a distinct time for centering, clearing, focusing, imagining; a time for pushing beyond, being playful, outrageous, heroic, probing; another phase for just looking, not yet judging, but becoming acquainted with the newly formed object. The thing needs time to be seen, examined in all its complexity, like a mother slowly looking at her new baby over and over again, each time discovering new details and new qualities. Ample time must be given to evaluation, but not at the beginning. When the enterprise has had sufficient time to run its course and display the mature phase of its potential, only then should the critical eye be cast.

Every new creative enterprise—as it unfolds, probes unknown terrain, and tests newly acquired strengths—is initially fragile. If the shadow of judgment falls too early and too heavily on barely emergent newness, it invariably finds it deficient. We must protect the emergent from the too-wise, too-informed eye of critical judgment. If not, we risk squashing awkward but promising shoots before they can develop to maturity.

BEYOND INTERPRETATION

An artistic endeavor comes into the world naked, unnamed, and vulnerable. Every creative effort requires the artist to wrest something from nothingness, a purposive cosmos from an apparently indifferent chaos. It is difficult and uncertain work. Initially the piece stands wobbly, often it is unclear whether it is the worst or the best piece we have made, whether it is empty of significance or full of a significance so new that it is all but impossible to read, its language wholly novel, its theme probing uncertain territory.

While the piece trembles in this protean state, an admirer comes along and declares, "I love it!" Before the rightful creator of the piece can find the means to bond with it, another arrives and preempts the rightful parents' love claim. What a confinement, what a collapse of possibilities!

You *do* love it? You find it worthy, meaningful to you? You identify so deeply and quickly with it, that on first sight you already love it? Yet I, its own parent, am still so tentative, still searching out the linkages between what this new thing is and all that I know to be. You map out its salient features before I see them, you value them before I do, you describe how the features of my own offspring reveal features of my inner self before I am able (willing?) to do so?

And now, seeing this new work of my own, this manifestation of my inner self *through your eyes,* named and valued *through your biography,* I can never see my own offspring raw and new. My perceptions must now and forever be filtered through yours. I must see my work through the veils of your words. Subtle, strange affiliations may be lost to me. New ranges of feelings may be lost to me. I am confined, biased by your good intentions.

Our art is really a chunk of ourselves. Everyone knows this. Love me, love my work. Love my work, and you love me. Withhold that love, you withhold from me your affection. I make some art things, and you say you love them. Great, you love my art, you love me. I'm lovable. This is good . . . so far.

Now, however, I'm back in my studio, scribbling and scrubbing away. And, as always, my little inner voice is chatting. "Gee, they really loved that last show. They really appreciated the way I used those blues and violets. They loved those deep moody evening landscapes with that severe palette, and they all remarked on the way black was used to give luminosity to those deeper tints of blue."

"I think I'll just try a few more." *Bam.*
"So I can't handle orange, eh? This will show them." *Bam.*
"I think I'll work in those lovely blues again." *Bam.*
"Virtuoso brush work, they said, virtuoso brush work!" *Bam.*
"These next landscapes are going to be just a bit ahead of my clientele, it'll give them something to reach for." *Bam.*
"That art critic from the *Times* said some nice things about my handling of line and that my work smacks of Diebenkorn—They ain't seen nothin' yet!" *Bam.*

Whose paintings are these now? Ours or our audience's? From whose wellspring are these images emerging, theirs or ours? At what depth of personal ambition are these products of our mind being generated? Whose dreams, whose stories are being told?

More insidious is the range of possible ideas, emotions, gestures, colors, lines that never emerge to the level of awareness as a consequence of "painting for admirers." All those idiosyncratic but possibly meaningful gestures that come fleetingly will be covered over. Because we will have such an urgency to make the lovable thing, things not lovable but meaningful will not get said. All those colors that lie dormant in our box and on our shelves will remain unopened because no one *else* seems to be interested in them.

All those dreams, fantasies, quirky ideas of ours will remain just dreams, and because they may be out of fashion, they will fade. Those dimensions of our being that are audacious, outrageous, searing, dark, giddy, profound rarely see the light of day because they stand opposed to propriety and it is along the threshold of propriety that much of our affection is won.

And so we become tamed by our need for affection, just as we tame others by its offering and withholding. The power of love to bind us is rewarding, but not when it binds us to convention or propriety, tames the vagaries of imagination, weakens the resolve. We must find a way to speak frankly about our work in such a fashion as to avoid reining in the scope of our creative potential.

Yet most often art criticism is a killing experience. We experience fear when speaking to others about our art; even worse, we fear having others speak about it. Our art is not a thing out there in the world, it is a creature of our own making, a manifestation of our self, just like our language or our ideas. Pointing out the inadequacies of one is to point out the deficiencies of the other. The phobia that many of us have about making art is mainly due, I believe, to having bad early experiences in which our art has been devalued by significant "others," with the corresponding sense of being personally devalued. "That's a very awkwardly drawn hand" means that there is an aspect of my performance, an aspect of me, which is awkward. "There is much too much blue in this section; it's killing this more delicate shade of brown over here" means I'm insensitive in two rather large categories of experience: color and placement. "Nothing is happening here, it's all so bland and unevocative that it lulls me to sleep" means I lull you to sleep, I am bland and unevocative. Even if the perceptions informing these statements are inaccurate, their debilitating effects are no less severe than they would be if they were accurate. If they are in fact inaccurate, they kill the spirit and mislead the mind. If there is substance to their judgments, they still kill the spirit, but more thoroughly, for the victim must acknowledge their accuracy and his or her own deficiency. These are the hobbling rewards of judgment for the artist. For the intrepid critic, I suppose the reward of offering one's bon mots is the satisfaction of being more sensitive than the other fellow. The superior aesthetic sensitivity of such people often blinds them to the devastating effects their comments may have.

It needn't be this way at all. We can make the exchange an extremely rewarding one for both parties, a dialogue that creates deeper levels of understanding, empathy, and mutual enlightenment. But to recast the processing of the creative enterprise, we must first seriously reexamine the effects that aesthetic judgments often have on the creative prowess of the artist for future enterprises.

All statements marking good and bad, like and dislike, in some fashion damage our spirit and consequently lead us to pull on our defensive armor. This is so because judgmental statements addressed our way force us into deferential posturing, timidity, and shallowness. If we are not forceful enough in our defense mechanisms we become psychically injured, anxious, feeling unattended and unrewarded for our efforts. This is a terribly steep price to pay for what is actually desired in the exchange: increased capacity for breadth of imagination and clarity of expression.

Devastating exchanges between artist and observer occur not only when aesthetic judgments are offered but also when the observer offers uninvited, intrusive insights into the psyche of the artist based merely upon a viewing of the artist's work, on the order of the following sample diagnoses: "I see by your impasto use of black and earthy browns, laid on with your hands, that you must be engaged in a return to primal processes. There is so much pain and torment in you, so much still to resolve." Or "These large sweeps of pale blue against the lime green wash are so ethereal. I too have the same carefree nature that you have. Your quiet self-assurance is something that I deeply admire." Unfortunately, you may not be ready to admit to your primal regressions (or they may not be regressions at all), and you may actually detest the person who so eagerly likens himself or herself to you. This type of intrusion in the psychic structure of the artist—without invitation and with scant evidence—is a costly exercise for both the artist and the critic. It is folly to presume to know the underlying personality of an artist by viewing any single work or even a more extensive body of work. And yet audiences usually find it fair game to guess how artists feel about life, art, themselves, their loved ones, God, and mankind. I wonder why it doesn't occur to these same knowledgeable souls that a good deal of art is play, still more of it is acting, some of it is experiment, some of it role playing, some of it fantasy, some of it borrowing, some teasing, some misleading, some candor, some blind searching, some catharsis, some mistakes, some serendipity, some in fact accurate transcriptions of the way things are. It's a complex business whose symbols are arcane and whose meanings are often obscure or purposefully obscured.

Much evidence is required to tease meaning from image; we make little of the enormity of the task by being quick here. Furthermore, information residing solely within the image is often woefully insufficient to the interpretation we seek. Certainly biographical or, better still, autobiographical information is a minimum requisite for any real analysis. And aside from the difficulty of determining the psyche of any artist based solely upon observing the work of art, such intrusion has other detrimental effects as well. You can be either correct or incorrect in your assessment. In either case, the

artist and the observer both suffer. If you are inaccurate, you are seen as insensitive, lacking in understanding, ignorant of essential material, weak in your judgment of character. The artist is offended by your inept description of his/her psyche, and, not without reason, becomes alienated from you, while you, as a consequence of being rebuffed for your efforts at interpretation, withdraw, feeling yourself to be seen as intrusive, insensitive, ignorant, careless, a poor judge of character.

64

If you are accurate in your interpretation, you again lose but in a different manner, in a different category of loss. If you are correct in your interpretation of the meaning residing within the piece, and the artist is still in the process of uncovering the meanings that reside there, you risk demonstrating your superior skill and consequently the perceptual deficiency of the artist. This creates a degree of tension between the artist and the interpreter, a dynamic asymmetry that must separate people perceived to be of unequal ability.

Although the momentary advantage of increased knowledge may be gained by an act of interpretation, the cost of acquiring this knowledge is great and long lasting. It leaves the artist dependent upon you for sources that must be claimed by the artist alone. This is especially pernicious for the artist, someone whose purpose it is to be independent of the judgments of others and whose task it is to create particular meaning from interior sources of feelings and ideas.

And so the content of the critical message may be accurate: you *did* put in too much blue, your hands *are* drawn clumsily, your compositions *are* bland—but these are perceptions one needs to be able to generate by oneself. If they are told to us directly by another, we have the answers before we know how to define the question and search for the answer. We also have the legacy of an injured spirit: "I require others to tell me what I should be able to see but cannot. Others are smarter than I am. I am dependent upon others to instigate my work and judge the quality of its execution. I am a person in need."

Art that serves the artist best is an experiment in expanding awareness. It is a display not so much of what is known and now portrayed as it is an investigation of what it is possible to know and of the effort necessary to convey those meanings in articulate and expressive ways to others. This is subtle stuff, subject to much rethinking and periods of silence. The work itself is the effort of reaching beyond what is presently in hand. The residue of this inquiry, the art "thing" does not necessarily contain the whole of the material that animated the endeavor. In short, the meanings of art are not obvious, the intentions of the artist even less so.

The whole of the matter is not merely that presuming to know the nature of the psyche of the artist is difficult; the point is that it is presumptuous and ultimately bruises the thing we wished exactly to spare—the creative spirit. This is not to say that the aesthetic sensibilities of others should not be shared or be put to the advantage of the artist. In fact, this is most important; the perspectives of others often can broaden the bases of our own, they can extend and sharpen our own personal repertoire of aesthetic criteria, deepen the expressiveness of our technique. And we can cultivate these sensibilities in others, but without the damages of judging and interpreting. We can do this by *describing* what we perceive and making that description personal and full. It is presumptuous to declare, upon viewing another's work, "Those are angry colors, those strokes are so violent. You must be feeling so tense and unhappy about yourself just now." There are no angry colors. There are only colors: blue, red, green, what have you. Colors don't contain feelings. People contain feelings, colors *provoke* feelings. And if certain colors provoke us to feel certain emotions, why not simply say so? In place of interpretation of others' assumed intentions and feelings, we can instead account for our experience of our own encounter with the work. Instead of speaking for someone else, we may substitute speaking for ourselves. "The colors that I see in this piece make me feel lighthearted, as if I'm floating without a care in the world. I feel as if a soft pastel cloud envelopes me, gently carrying me to safe and welcoming places."

Notice how these latter statements account only for the experiences of the speaker. They do not presume to speak for the maker of the piece, nor do they presume to know that person's mind. The statements only account for the personal reactions of the viewer upon encountering the work of another. In this way there is no poking about uninvited in another's mind. There is no risk of being right or wrong, because we are only speaking about our own reactions. The act of perception on our part, filtered through our unique autobiography, results in our own idiosyncratic responses. Artists are always interested and informed by the reactions our work has on our audience. We are not so interested in having our audience peeping into our minds.

Suppose there is actually a similarity between what the artist intended to portray in the piece and how the piece made someone else feel. Wonderful! Now we have much to talk about and explore. Suppose there is no similarity between what the artist intended and the viewer's experience on viewing it. Wonderful! Now we have much to talk about and explore. The first instance is significant because there is a reinforcing and affirming of mutually held perceptions. The former is signifcant because there is an expansion of perception as a result of new territories being surveyed that were heretofore unseen, even unseeable without the news from the other side.

NEITHER JUDGMENT NOR INTERPRETATION: DESCRIPTION

We all need to be seen and listened to. Even if there is no advice offered, solace proffered, or claims of affection, at least let us be attended to. "Attention, attention must be paid," cries Willy Loman's wife on the fading of her Willy in *Death of a Salesman*. So it is with art and artists.

Most of us go through life believing that no one really understands us. And frankly, that's probably accurate. In some real sense we feel alone not because people don't love us or respect us, but because who they love and who they respect is not really the person we know ourselves to be. So their love and respect, as precious and as necessary as it is, usually rings untrue.

Before there can be the love that satisfies, the respect that quenches all inner uncertainty, there must be full and undivided attention paid to the object of our love. Seeing the other fully, fully affirms the other. Paying close and undivided attention to the other demonstrates that that person is worth being paid attention to, that there is worth to his or her very presence. Offering a full account of what is seen in our work demonstrates that we have been heard, someone has finally seen us for who we are. This is a rare and welcome good.

The following hypothetical dialogue represents an exchange between an artist and a mentor employing description without judgment, a process that helps to clarify issues for the artist.

Artist and companion are looking at a work just completed.

Artist: This seemed very moving to me as I made it, and does so even now as I look at it. But I'm so deeply enmeshed in it, the whole thing is beginning to get confused. I began with certain intentions, and somewhere through the thing it seemed to get away from me. I've brought it back, but I'm not sure just what I did bring back. My eyes are tired, I'm not seeing it clearly any more. I wonder what *you* see.

Viewer: Well, let me just talk out loud and tell you what I see as my seeing unravels. (*Long pause while viewer slowly scans the work.*) I guess I see two main things. This great big sweep of white mist, like an ice cloud ascending over these three deeper bands or phases. My eyes keep turning first to these underlying phases. The one on the left is painted with a velocity and broad length of stroke that the others do not exhibit. The dives and sweeps of your brush seem to dance that bluish purple all over the place. The strokes ascend and curl back on themselves, like rising smoke, or even cold flames. The middle phase seems more composed, even stately in its stroke. The spaces are more regular. They also ascend, but are more deliberate, controlled, and less brassy and dancey. The color seems more complex, many more hues and tints are intermingled here. It has a bit of a softness, too, that the other phase lacks. Now let's look at the right side. The largest of the three seems the most ethereal. I can't make out the individual colors anymore, but I sense their presence. This phase has the softest, yet the deepest degree of space, it bleeds off the paper to the right and above, even at the bottom. There seems to be no direction to the strokes, but a gentle floating about. It appears to be spreading out, rather than stationary. Shall I go on?

Artist: Yes, please do.

Viewer: The white mist appears to me as a crystal cloud, spreading over all three underpinning phases. This area has a tremendous degree of activity. It's painted, dry-brushed, smeared, spattered, dappled, yet in sum, it's cloud-like, overspreading all beneath. Gently, not weighing down or obliterating, it covers all the rest like a thin sheet of gauze. It sweeps from left to right, from bottom to top, in this gently upward thrusting arc. It combines the lower three phases and somehow makes the individual parts coalesce as parts of a whole. The ice cloud completes the three underlying phases by weaving them into a larger theme.

At the moment, without the benefit of some sign from you, this is about as far as I can go.

Artist: Good, you've said some things that help me to think this through in a less muddled way than before. Thanks. You know, as I was working on this, I don't remember pausing between the three vertical forms and that white misty form. So in my mind, they were just four forms, three going one way, one the other. But as you spoke of what you saw, you tended to separate these forms into two categories, an underlayment and a superimposition. Now when I look at the painting this distinction seems real and to grow in importance. There is a dynamic tension or resistance, not really a struggle but some kind of battle going on here. I'll have to think more about just what that battle is really like and between whom.

You called this white, mistlike form here an ice or crystal cloud, something like that. For me that connotes cold, and I don't feel temperature at all in this image. If anything, I like its neutrality, it's there but unobtrusive. That's the way it feels, smooth, just lightly touching down. . . . It's clearer to me now, but you know, it wasn't clear at all as I was making it. Now, seeing the work after hearing you traverse the same territory, sort of singing out the points of interest along the way, the whole of the story seems to come together a bit more. I mean, there it is, the past, the present, the future, each with its own story, its own choreography and music. And over them all, that ice mist, as you called it, is what may be my spirit or soul, the thing that moves me on. I'll have to spend some time looking at this, chewing on your observation, walking over these bumps and valleys again. Thanks for your care.

The above exchange is admittedly a forced and condensed version of what in reality would be more drawn out, more hesitant, involving more of an exchange. Nonetheless it is offered in this form to demonstrate how description alone serves the artist in clarifying images that have often been generated from subliminal levels and therefore precede any rational synthesis.

A more forceful exchange between artist and viewer is the clarifying inquiry. In this mode, the viewer takes a more active role in guiding the exchange. Not judging or opining but mirroring, testing, challenging the artist's assertions in order to accelerate the process of acquainting the conscious mind with the wisdom of the subconscious material as expressed in images. The intent here is to enable the artist to become more overtly familiar with the associative meanings of his or her imagery.

Our task, then, is to act as a midwife, to help the artist comprehend, decode what is already there but resides within the tacit dimension. We are not interested here in leading questions or questions put in rhetorical format. Such formulations only confine the artist to think along lines already laid out by the questioner. What we are interested in are queries that can deepen and broaden the artist's own associations with the work. As I mentioned earlier, the meeting of one's rational, discursive mind with one's subliminal and gestural mind can lead to a most empowering alliance, whereby the wisdom of both minds can bring that wisdom to bear on a variety of settings, to the somatic and subliminal and to the rational and deliberate.

The following dialogue is intended to illustrate how this mode of clarifying inquiry sounds. The artist has recently completed work on a painting and brings it to the attention of a companion. There is already in place an established sense of trust between the two.

A meditative, quizzical look on her face, the artist initiates the dialogue.

Artist: I don't know about this image, something is there, something is tugging at me here, but . . . I don't know.

Companion: Tugging at you? What kind of feeling is that for you?

Artist: When I was working on the piece, I began to feel an increase of energy, excitement, but somewhere along the way I felt it slipping . . . slipping away from me.

Companion: Can you point out the portion of the image that still retains that initial energy, excitement?

Artist: Well, it's a bit layered over now, but it was here, in this area, this boxlike form enclosing this little bit of blue.

Companion: This box of gray bars, enclosing this pale blue?

Artist: Yes, the gray box keeping the blue in.

Companion: Can you recollect the feelings, sensations you experienced when you were initially making the gray space, keeping the blue enclosed?

Artist: At first it was simply automatic, but not something that I had ever done before. Then I began to get into those gray bars, it felt right to press down, deliberately forming them one after the other, slowly, even a little sadly. Then it seemed I just had to use that blue, that pale, warm blue in the center, it seemed to throb with a kind of life, a . . . I don't know, but it seemed very necessary.

Companion: The blue felt necessary for you, in what way?

Artist: In what way, in what way is blue necessary, pale blue, warm blue, soft, flat, warm blue necessary . . .

(After a long and necessary silence)

Companion: What is there in your life that speaks of soft, flat, warm blue?

Artist: Hope, maybe hope, summer days, carefree summer days.

Companion: Just any hope?

Artist: No, not just any hope, hope in my accepting myself, hope in accepting my color, my femininity, hope—I don't know, in my—oh, no, really I think it's hope that my spirit remains uncrushed, still there after all these years.

Companion: Your pale blue spirit, hopefully still alive.

Artist: Yes, that feels right. My pale blue spirit.

Companion: And the gray area?

Artist: Yes, the gray! (*spoken softly*) The gray, the gray bars, squeezing in, pressing in the pale blue.

Companion: Whose gray is that?

Artist: I don't know, the world's, I guess. Maybe the world.

Companion: The world? Your world? Whose world?

Artist: You know, it's not the world, I'm just bullshitting myself here. It's me. The gray is me too, really, it's me.

Companion: What aspect of you is gray?

Artist: It's not just gray, its gray bars, or stripes. No, it's really gray fences.

Companion: The gray fences in your blue?

Artist: No, it's not that feeling. The gray is more like a window frame. It frames the blue, it sets a boundary to it, like the inside and the outside.

Companion: The inside of what or who, the outside of what?

Artist: I need that gray window frame to set some kind of boundary to that blue stuff, or I'll stay in that wild blue yonder forever. I'll never come inside. I'll float off to who knows where.

Companion: And the gray without the blue?

Artist: Is just civilized, just a nice, good kid, who loves everything she's supposed to, and doesn't do anything she's not supposed to. I need this gray, and I want more of this blue.

Companion: The blue and the gray.

Artist: The blue and the gray.

We have followed this dialogue to the point where the artist had begun to decode a portion of her subliminal language and to appreciate some of its associative meanings. As a consequence of this dialogue, the artist has an expanded personal association with two primal colors, colors she now can speak with and about authoritatively. Not just gray or blue: these particular tints and shades of gray and blue. She can also speak in flat planes and bars, with a heightened sense of their particular meaningfulness. The colors and shapes explored in this work take on a more vivid personality, a particular biography, an expressive naturalness. How these colors and shapes are graphic displays of inner psychic structures seems also somewhat clearer for her now.

We can proceed still further with our artist and provide additional impetus to her expressive empowerment. To do so we might continue the dialogue in a number of other directions, by asking questions such as the following:

- What prompted you to scribble those white lines on top of those other colors? I see that on the left-hand side, the blue and gray background is overlayered with white, almost scribbled marks. (This to explore her resistance to the crucial theme of blue and gray.)
- What would it be like if you entered the arena of this same theme, approaching this again in paint, but this time bringing to the encounter your present understandings? (This to further clarify and affirm her newfound identifications.)
- I wonder if you have assayed all the possibilities of your blueness and grayness. What might happen if you just played with these colors and strokes further to see what happens? (This to invite further exploration of what is at the moment a barely formed relationship.)
- This overlaying, almost but not quite concealing the blue and the gray, as you look at it now, what's that about? (This to pick up on the other theme of the image, which was used to "bail her out" of the weightiness of the primary theme. Obviously, this second theme is very powerful for her in that it was able to divert her from a major personal and graphic event.)
- You know, I admire the courage you just showed to look so unflinchingly at your own work, to set aside the easy baloney that you certainly could

have stayed with, and to share this stuff with me. I appreciate that. (Not gratuitously, nor in a pat way, but to honestly acknowledge that you, the inquirer, were witness to a creative act requiring honesty, acceptable vulnerability, and integrity, and that you were allowed to share in it.)

Notice how the bonds of partnering were woven here without any judgment about good and bad, without affection given or withheld, without intrusive commentary on what *you* think she thinks or feels, and without usurping her right to be the first person to come to know and love her own work. Acquainting our own rational selves with the products of our creative-intuitive expressions is, as we have just seen, neither automatic nor easy.

We said earlier that the hand cannot lie, meaning that as the hand leaves its mark upon the page, there is unmistakable and unconcealable evidence of choice of color, texture, line, stroke, and so on. The hand leaves its trail sometimes subtly, sometimes too boldly, prompted by the urgencies of our inner life. But the trail is not a conspicuous one directly illustrating our interior motivations. Any language, verbal or visual, is a complex system of symbols representing states of mind, requiring that both the speaker and the respondent understand how to make and decode these symbols. Even so, native speakers of the same language often have serious difficulty communicating. Witness the tiffs between marriage partners, friends, siblings, statesmen—really, everyone. Not only is there difficulty in communicating interpersonally, there is also difficulty in communicating intrapsychically. That is, the fact that we create our symbols from deep and personal sources does not necessarily mean we know how to decipher these same symbols.

I've spoken elsewhere about the fact that we seem to have two minds at work. One mind utters a thought that emerges from our subconscious, using highly idiosyncratic signs and symbols. The other mind is our rational and public mind, which partakes of a common linguistic heritage but as of yet is unfamiliar with the language being uttered by its own intuitive partner. Freud, of course, recognized this phenomena of our double-mindedness, which he referred to as the conscious and the subconscious, and posited that the ultimate goal of psychotherapy was to acquaint the conscious mind with the material of the subconscious mind and so make the psyche whole.

It is strange that our brain can generate two or more minds, each with its distinctive way of knowing and speaking. But this is no stranger, I suppose, than the existence of our waking mind and our dreaming one, one bounded by the inexorable constraints of time, space, gravity, causality, the other oblivious to all those elements as constraints, employing them instead as expressive media. And just as our dream mind "speaks" in a langauge foreign— sometimes alarmingly foreign—to our wakeful mind, so does our subliminal mind often make poignant remarks that are obscure to our rational mind, even in our wakeful state.

A major objective of this book is to reconsider the actual functions of art to include reacquainting our rational discursive mind with the meanings of the symbols uttered by its intuitive counterparts. This primary goal of psychoanalysis was particularly important in the work of Carl Jung and Otto Rank, who both related the creative process to therapy along lines that Freud pursued less forcefully and clearly. In this text the creative process is employed with different emphasis and distinctly different means from those utilized by psychotherapists; the goal, however, is similar: to make us whole, more thoroughly alive, and more able to express a fuller degree of creative vitality.

Our ambition, generally speaking, has been to free up the available energies that are currently locked up in old ineffectual ways. It requires effort to face the person we are but no longer wish to remain. It requires effort to try on new ways—even though we believe we may prefer them—when we don't yet know what they may feel like or what price we may have to pay for their as yet uncertain rewards. The strategies we will employ next have been designed to enable us to carry out the following transformational tasks:

- to affirm, through practice, new ways of looking and responding
- to discard the many-layered masks that we use to conceal the person we actually are
- to fathom and celebrate in public the person we really are
- to locate our natural "voice," its rhythm, tone, and melody, so that the "songs" we sing flow easily with conviction and with heart
- to assume responsibility for the creation of the life we desire, and give up the comfortable role of victim of circumstances

These tasks are all demanding. Since the way we are is in large measure the way we are with others and as a consequence of others, it is particularly empowering to undertake these exercises in the company of others. In facing the subtle task of decoding the tacit meanings embedded in original imagery, working in partnership or in small groups has several advantages over working entirely on one's own.

Often it is not the maker of a piece but others who first notice the emergent signs of an original mark, color, gesture. All newness is fragile; having someone besides us notice the features of the new and reflect them back to us imparts a certain substance and in-the-worldness to the new. Now at least *two* people have seen it, and two people witnessing something are less likely to miss its details than if it is seen only by one. Things seen by only one observer, when they are extreme in their divergences from the norm, in their fleeting presence, in their subtlety or complexity, are all too easy to pass over, so that the potential impact of the event is often reduced to something elusive, to a mere figment of imagination.

All utterance is in some way a confession. "Here is where I stand, this is my truth, this is the best I can do." What is the redemptive power of a confession with no one there to hear it? Speaking is only one half of language; someone else listening is the other half.

The end of art is not art, but communication, or better still communion, breaking out of the solitariness and silence of one dimension of ourselves and making contact with the "other." That other may be intrapsychic: the conscious mind acknowledging the subconscious; or it may be interpsychic: one person meeting another; or it may even be transpersonal: one self touching the universe.

SEEKING AND FINDING THE WORLD: A FINAL WORD TO THE JOURNEYMAN

Our culture places a high value on being busy. We like busy people; they always seem so determined, so preoccupied. It seems it almost doesn't matter *what* they are doing, as long as they look busy and have things in order. Some of these hyperactive types seek and manage to acquire many things: a lot of money, a lot of power, a lot of shoes, cars, collectibles, what have you. They are successful. Photos of successful business executives always show them with a telephone in one hand and an expensive pen in the other: very busy, on to the next deal. And, of course much *is* gained by active seeking—but not everything. Some things come to us as a consequence not of seeking, but by patience and a quiet open hand.

Those who do put a great deal of energy into the chase often feel that unless they pursue, they will not get. That's what keeps them hopping about so madly. There is a kind of desperation in their pursuit of nice things, a kind of breathless anxiety accompanying their quest: Will I get it? I'll die if I don't get it! Ostensibly that search is for cars, shoes, power, friends, but beneath the material need may exist a frightening emptiness brought about by a weak sense of self-esteem, poor boundary definition, a sense of being unloved and unlovable. The drive to acquire is the classic case of adult compensation for early deprivation, as portrayed so vividly in the movie *Citizen Kane.*

Convert this scenario from life adventures to creative adventures, and the same dynamics apply. When we feel existentially empty, denied, hungry in life, we will move that same way across our canvas or stage or blank page. The work reflects our preoccupation with success. We have our eyes and heart and hand not on what we are doing, but elsewhere on some distant goal: the show, the compliment, the sale, the glowing review. Not fully present or in touch with our own actions, uncomfortable in our own minds and dissatisfied with our current station in life, we become a self divided.

Our work becomes forced, self-conscious, pretentious. It lacks the natural grace of an uncomplicated mind and a calm spirit. Such existential hunger covered over by material pursuits is a deep-seated state of mind that requires heroic countermeasures to overcome. We may address this issue by experimenting with the following alternative set of propositions.

At the beginning of this book I likened the world to a great stream rushing inexorably past and around us. We don't create this stream; it is already here and full to bursting. This stream is the universe, made up of a zillion teeming things, endlessly, unpredictably tumbling and wooshing by. Yet we can do something more than anxiously thrash about or passively allow everything to float past us. To use the term *suffer* in its older sense, we can suffer the world to come to us. And surprisingly, it does. Not—in fact, never—the way we would have it, but come to us it will. And it is the openness of our minds that enables us to "catch" it.

Of this openminded engagement with the world, Martin Buber has said the following:

> The *Thou* meets me through grace—it is not found by seeking. But my speaking of the primary word to it is an act of my being, is indeed *the* act of my being.
> The *Thou* meets me. But I step into direct relation with it. Hence the relation means being chosen and choosing, suffering and action in one; just as any action of the whole being, which means the suspension of all partial actions and consequently of all sensations of actions grounded only in their particular limitation, is bound to resemble suffering.
> The primary word *I–Thou* can be spoken only with the whole being. Concentration and fusion into the whole being can never take place through my agency, nor can it ever take place without me. I become through my relation to the *Thou*; as I become *I,* I say *Thou.* [25]

To confront the evolving canvas-stage-page in this frame of mind is to permit our hand and imagination a wide tether, to generate a welter of material from deep inside and from way out there. The trick is not to grab onto the first thing that comes our way and to trust that the flow won't dry up. If we do grab onto the first thing, fix our eye on a single item, all our energies are expended in holding onto it, while the rest of the flotsam blurs and the force behind the stream seems to diminish. By contrast, the more we allow the stream to pour out or wash over us, the more of it there seems to be. In this eager, expectant state, the stream of consciousness flows deepest. Rollo May has clarified the difference between creative receptivity and passivity in a passage that sheds further light on the state I am referring to here.

> The receptivity of the artist must never be confused with passivity. Receptivity is the artist's holding him- or herself alive and open to hear what being

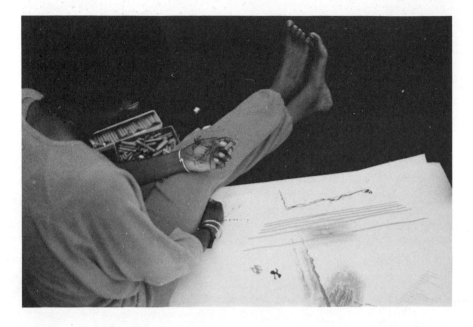

may speak. Such receptivity requires a nimbleness, a fine-honed sensitivity in order to let one's self be the vehicle of whatever vision may emerge. . . .

It is necessary for the birthing process to begin to move in its own organic time. It is necessary that the artist have this sense of timing, that he or she respect these periods of receptivity as part of the mystery of creativity and creation.[26]

Instead of always pursuing the world, we may on occasion allow the world to be generated spontaneously from the natural activity of our mind and the natural, inexorable flow of the universe. Night will come in due course. The moon will rise on schedule. Spring with its billions of expanding things will follow on the crystals of winter. Life will hiss, buzz, and pop all around us, whether we seek it or not. And on schedule: *its* schedule, not ours. The world already is most emphatically here and happening. It was here before us and came through the last billions of years quite well without us. The world is quite present, quite large and available. It is the limitations we have placed upon our minds that obscure the world and close off our access to what already is ours.

The preceding chapters proposed the general point of view that the creative process is natural and inborn and has the potential not only of transforming the page or canvas into something desired but, more important, of enhancing our quality of life. But how to actually *do* this? The following chapters offer specific guidance in how to shape our artistic endeavors so that they actualize this transformative potential. I have used the term *Creative Encounter* to describe the process by which an engagement with art is employed for both personal and expressive growth. The principles of designing these Creative Encounters are the subject of the next chapter.

3

Designing Creative Encounters

THE NATURE OF THE ENCOUNTER: INTRODUCTORY REMARKS

Art is a response to a call.

The nature of the call determines to a large extent the nature of the response. The call is an invitation, a challenge to engage with the world in such a manner that an increase of creative expression in life and art is the ultimate reward. Each call is an invitation to step forward, to cut more deeply into life, to aspire to grander ambitions, to relinquish our hold on the past, and to open our hand to the future.

The call begins with an invitation to participate in a creative encounter, a challenge whose nature is such that the only place to turn to for its exploration is inward. No borrowed answer will do because no one other than yourself could possibly "know" the answer. The effort to respond fully to the engagement sharpens perception, opens the eyes, increases the ambition to engage ever deeper and broader issues, and infuses subsequent efforts with vitality.

How to proffer the invitation in such a manner so as not to intimidate and therefore discourage? How to propose the engagement so that any genuine response offers genuine reward? Many characteristics of creative encounters have a decided effect on the quality of the response and maximize personal and creative profit. The following pages explore the principles upon which our encounters are designed, beginning with a discussion of the general ambiance within which these encounters take place. It is a context similar to the social and psychic context of transformative rituals, and our discussion will therefore begin with the uses of ritual in transformative experiences.

ELEMENTS OF TRANSFORMATIVE RITUALS

If we step back from the particular story line of such rituals of transformation as confirmation, marriage, or election to high office and examine their underlying structure, we will notice certain similar patterns throughout. By "structure of a ritual" I mean the distinctive events that the novice undergoes in order to attain the status, privileges, and obligations associated with that ritual.

A transformative ritual is a means by which the individual eventually dies to a significant element of his or her past life and accedes to a new and elevated position. Any major transition requires a shifting of the psychic components of our life. This period of disequilibrium brings with it varying degrees of stress. The usual reaction to stress is a defensive attempt to preserve what is possessed and known. Transformative rituals must circumvent this natural and often appropriate defensive use of energies because preserving that which is already in place is precisely what is not desired. We can design events so as to limit these reactions in several ways. Like the initiates of any rites of passage, we can "soften" our hold on or system of beliefs about those conceptions of self we wish to alter. We cannot, for example, be elevated to the status of full adulthood if we maintain our identity as dependent children; we cannot successfully accept the role of husband or wife while holding to the mores and self-conception of a single individual.

To soften our self-conceptions is not to abandon completely the person we were, not is it to deny the legitimacy of those ideas and attendant behaviors. To soften our belief system is to soften the boundary definition of those conceptions so that other emergent conceptions can repattern the contours of our lives. In particular, we are interested in softening our conception of two definitions that determine so much of our behavior as artists: that of the term *art* and that of *beauty*. In chapter 1 we examined both terms and looked at alternative ways of conceiving them. Here I will briefly reiterate those earlier arguments. If we are not to be fixated by the term *art*, confined by our past associations and experiences with it and all it confers, infers, allows, and disallows, we must thrust our attention forward, become interested in the series of encounters and self-discoveries through which we will create our personal meaning of *art*. In spite of everything we already "know" about the history of art, we must will ourselves to be in some substantial sense the first person to claim the title of artist.

The term *beauty* must similarly be examined and redefined. Here again our familiarity with the canons of good form can only serve us as gates of perception. If we are to broaden those gates, even breach the walls, we must break the spell that conventional canons of beauty hold over us. Determination is needed here, for the allure of what we have been predisposed to find beautiful is real and powerful. We have to become disenchanted with its appearance. We have to train ourselves to note the classically formed thing with as much curiosity as we turn our attention to any other expressive, compelling form. How do you do that? Simply do it. Each time you catch yourself slipping back to conventional ways of seeing, consciously will yourself to shift focus. As you deliberately practice this way of seeing, you will be emboldened in your efforts because you know that if you remain fascinated by conventional beauty you will remain exactly where you are, and that's not what you want for yourself.

If we can first soften, then extend the boundary definition of these two terms, we will have created a mental climate within which a surprising range of novel perceptions may occur. This is the first phase of the transformative ritual: opening, then broadening, the gates of perception.

Daring to Be New

To insure that the gates of perception remain open, we need to suspend our interest in forming aesthetic judgments concerning things that pass before our eyes. I have described earlier how such judgments are pernicious both for the creator and for the audience in that they divert us from the more serious and difficult task of bending our efforts toward the creation of significant expression. Aesthetic judgments, especially those made early in the creative enterprise, often bias the outcome in the direction of making likeable things rather than honest and searching things. Likeability is nice, but it's not what we need here and now. Here we seek to support the self in the precarious state of evolving. The climate for the nurturance of a self evolving is one that allows that self to try on many new ways, slowly, deliberately, playfully, out of judgment's harsh reach.

At the outset of our transformation, things are raw and uncertain. Arriving at judgment early is to evaluate the new against criteria imparted from the past. (Where else could it come from?) At the outset of any undertaking, especially one of major renovation, we are just beginning to expand our range of aspirations and to test our mettle. During this opening phase our efforts are best devoted to designing the experiment, tinkering with the equipment, daring ourselves to consider new thoughts. This is not the time to give attention over to calculating our chances of success or crafting our results. Nor is this the time to pass judgment on our efforts. This is a phase of our encounter with becoming in which the excitement of first-time adventure is to be savored. It's better not to have anyone watching as we bumble through these first, necessary steps.

On Not Knowing

Another quality of mind that will further our purpose of creating an open frame of reference is our acknowledgment of the legitimacy of Not Knowing—not knowing what is about to take place, not knowing in advance anything about ourselves, our partners, the piece of paper that we face, even the "point" of the exercise at hand. Our usual response to any real sense of not knowing is to shrink back from the encounter. As a consequence, we are likely to fall back upon tried ways, disengage with the actual circumstances we find ourselves in, and rerun past scenarios. The failure to make contact with the reality we are in causes us in turn to feel out of our element and disempowered. In this dispirited state we certainly do not feel in a mood for creative play or adventures of the imagination.

We want to claim the positive utility of the Not Knowing frame of mind and not permit it to be an impediment to full engagement in creative activities. Instead of allowing Not Knowing to paralyze forward progress, we can see Not Knowing as a frame of mind which occurs at the boundary line between all that is known and all that is yet to be known. The only point of departure into the unknown, into transformative possibilities, is at this very zone that borders on the known and unknown. This is the fruitful departing edge for all adventures that lead to discovery.

"Knowing" is having all the pieces of the map in place and traversing familiar grounds. Not Knowing is to appreciate that what you do know is limited and circumscribed by what you have yet to know. Of course there is excitement here, even anxiety, but conceive it as the excitement of an appetite ready to be satisfied rather than the impending falling off the edge of the world.

Not Knowing is also a humble state of mind. Aware of its own incompleteness, it realizes that it is still open to instruction and improvement. This seems a more accurate description of the way we are than the notion that in fact all is finished with us and that we do know all that it is necessary to know.

Finally, a state of Not Knowing allows us greater facility in rearranging what we know into new configurations and definitions of reality. In this way, the mind-set of Not Knowing can be seen as the prerequisite state of mind for creative play, which in turn sets the stage for transformational endeavors. Rather than fearing Not Knowing, we might welcome that break in our mind's defenses, for it is at this tear in the seams of our worldview that newness enters.

Here are some reflections on the powers and effects of Not Knowing; feel free to add your own.

- Not Knowing is the pregnant silence around which the world turns.
- It is the zero point from which new things spring.
- When all is empty, all is ready.
- The new must wait until the past is gone to make its appearance.
- Knowing what you do know is good. Acknowledging what you don't know is also good. Appreciating where one leaves off and the other begins is very good.

- Trust, not assurance, glides us past what we know, enabling us to tumble into the new. When trust is insufficient, we still have faith to carry us further on.
- Fear is the symptom indicating that great things are being confronted, the boundaries of what we take to be safe, real, and good.
- Fear creates a wall. When confronted by a feared thing, we encapsulate ourselves, just as viruses and soldiers do when things are not going well. With fear of the unknown compelling us, we break off contact with external reality and subcreate a smaller, safer enclosure, intended to be a temporary haven while the killing winds pass. This is OK. No one ought to be outside in such weather. But when the weather lets up, and we *still* remain behind shuttered walls, that's when problems arise. No longer is it the harmful ephemeral "thing out there" that keeps us cloistered; now our memories and imaginations imprison us. We forget that it was a passing storm that frightened us. We then generalize from this episode and thus create a whole climate of inhibitions. Finally, we dwell there, sometimes for the rest of our life.
- We must learn to discriminate between when the wind is blowing and when our memory is howling. We must take courage to breach the walls we have built to keep out the real dangers and test whether they are still present or have gone their ways. And when it ceases to howl outside, we must have the wherewithal to let it also go from our minds and turn to the new day.
- Not Knowing need not engender fearful reactions precipitating the shutdown and withdrawal of our contact with the world. Instead, rename it the pregnant silence, and in this way lay claim to the place around which the world turns and makes itself new.

Bearing Witness

Much of language is used to portray how the world looks and feels from where we happen to be. Sometimes we use language in a competitive manner, to display our superiority or to defend ourself against someone else's display of superiority. At other times we become clever, eloquent beyond necessity, we posture this way and that in order to gain favor, to somehow win more than we had before. Like the howling of wolves or the chatter of birds, such use of language is a declaration of territoriality, a signing of status, a warning or a beckoning call. These are important and necessary functions of language. But they set us against the world, as if there weren't enough room or resources for all of us, as if the elevation of my status were dependent upon the suppression of yours.

According to this mind-set, others are potential adversaries who seek their own advancement at our cost. Our reaction to this perceived assault is to armor ourselves, to use our first line of defense—language—to test the measure of our adversary and calculate our path of survival or (hopefully) of success. We duel with life, always anxious about the outcome. How can a mind so preoccupied with survival be open to new, fragile possibilities? How can we play in such dangerous streets?

I don't think we can. We must find a way to be in the world that allows us to break out of this conceptual arena of discord. We must find a way to speak to each other in the belief that there is enough room for all. We must suppose this. Yes, it is naive; yes, there are a million reasons to be defensive and combative, and they are not imaginary.

So: we have a choice. We can remain defensive, combative, and maintain the world as it is and has been. Or we can see what happens if we take that leap past what we know into the possible arena of communion, where we meet to share and not to win. That sounds like a rather minor achievement: "to share." And to give up winning for sharing may appear more dubious still. But let us examine for a moment what is gained by doing so.

For one thing, rather than employ our energies to construct endlessly elaborate battlements within which we breathlessly survive, or to design engines of combat with which to conquer the world, we might instead simply touch the world. I mean touch the real world. I mean actually make contact with the living, immense, stunning world.

Can you get just a glimmer of what that would be like? Has that ever happened to you? Have you ever felt not alone? Have you ever sensed that you were seen not by other people but something alive in the universe, and that you were OK? Has something wild ever come up to you, touched you, and not fled? Have you ever lain down at night in an open field—no tent, no fire, no companions—and slept easily under the star-spangled sky, cushioned only by the patient earth? Have you ever felt unafraid, as if you belonged here, as if you too were as natural and wild as a deer, a stone, a pine? Do you know the grace of expression, the range of imagination that this sense of belonging engenders? This is what may be ours when we face the world not as adversaries but as communicants.

When we are no longer preoccupied with defending and offending, the same energies that were put to the service of self-protection are now available for the creation of ways to touch and be touched by the world. And as we create an ever-wider palette of such points of contact, we extend the scope of our awareness, deeper, wider, lighter. That is what we want: the transformation of the person we are into the person we desire to be.

How to recast our use of language from combat to communion? I have

spoken before about the possibility of describing rather than judging or measuring. I'd like to substitute another term here for *description,* one that is more dynamic and potent; I mean *bearing witness.*

Bearing witness, like any creative act, is a willful expression of what it feels like to be yourself. It is a simple act and at the same time a courageous one. You speak for yourself and you speak of yourself. You tell your own story. Instead of claiming knowledge of others as in the statement *"When people see* the color blue, *they experience* a calming effect," Bearing Witness more simply but courageously declares, *"When I see* certain shades of brown, *I begin to feel* heavy, slow, somehow closed in." Instead of speaking in the third person indefinite (*"People are slow* to anger about social injustices to minorities"), Bearing Witness speaks in the first person: *"Greens upset me!* There isn't a green that sits well with me, no matter what the shade. Green always reminds me of vegetables on my plate." Instead of speaking from hearsay (*"Van Gogh was such* an intense person"), Bearing Witness claims to speak only of what we know directly: "Van Gogh's painting *The Night Café evokes in me* the most destabilizing feelings. I can't seem to find the painting's center point. I begin to shift my own equilibrium point all over the place to get in sync with the painting, and I can never do it."

Instead of accusing others of causing us to have particular feelings (*"You make me* so happy"), Bearing Witness takes full responsibility for what is occurring within: "*I feel so pleased* when I see you turning in my direction."

Bearing Witness, in speaking only of ourself and for ourself, allows everyone else to do likewise without anyone feeling misunderstood, for no one is claiming to have understood anyone else. No one feels in the minority because no one claims any constituency for their perceptions. No one feels judged because there is no external and absolute standard against which anyone's statement can be judged. Statements are understood as being accounts of the news from unique points in the universe. Bearing Witness is indisputable, and therefore there are no grounds for dispute. Bearing Witness always draws from within, always makes the speaker the world's only expert on the subject. The authority of Bearing Witness resides in its humility, in its speaking only of and for itself. What it speaks of may reflect a restricted range, but its truths are unshakable and their expression unusually sound.

Deceit and guile can corrupt any intention, of course, and they can do the same here. We can only invite meeting and provide opportunities for encounters of large moment. We will do this if we say we are interested in portraying our own truths and attending to others who do likewise. This may be the closest we can get to touching and being touched by the human portion of the world. This shift in language from winning to sharing—perhaps done at first mechanically or, we might say in this instance, ritualistically—eventually sets in motion a corresponding shift in consciousness. This in turn invites deeper, more authentic expression. And that is what we desire.

Being There

One final thing that we can do to "open" the arena of creative expression is to "be there" fully for others when they make the significant effort to share themselves in some way with us. Attentive, full turning toward another who reaches out in our direction may sound like something we do ordinarily whenever anyone addresses us, but do we really? I think not. Test it. Watch yourself as you listen to someone else to see how much attention you can focus on them and how much on yourself. Watch your fidgeting, the rehearsing of what you will say in anticipation of their completion of their statement. Once seen, it is unsettling how uninterested we actually are in anyone other than ourselves. This ordinary way of relating to others will serve us poorly in our ambition to make creative encounters more than an entertainment. If it is transformation we want, this degree of full living requires full meetings, full support, and utter concern. We have to break out of our isolation and self-fascination and to turn, fully, to the other. Really see who is out there. Really try to listen without interior or exterior commentary. Attempt to see everything, hear every word, every inflection, every breath, every silence. Hear not only with your ears, but with your skin, your fingers, your heart. Focus your available energy in the direction of the other and surround that person with your care. That's being there. There are many books on the art of cultivating more effective listening and communication skills.* Here let me simply call attention to the need for our being there for our partners in our fullest, most attentive stance.

The result of being present, not necessarily offering wise counsel or consolation or anything other than full, undivided, *patient* attention, is an encouragement of full and honest expression. No need for partial revelations, timidity, or shallow thought and feeling. Being there for the other encourages what we mutually desire: greater creative expression, and thus greater transformation.

You Are Both Agent and Subject of Change

An element found in rituals that we can employ for transformative purposes is the fact that all participants in the activity are both agents of change and the subject of change. Most often in our society we conduct ourselves in such a manner as to maximize our own profit, our private rewards. The focus on private gain, whatever else it brings about, also causes a substantial degree of competitiveness and hoarding. This sequestering of resources, this private achievement, indifferent as it is to the success of one's peers, breeds an atmosphere of hositility, anxiety, and selfishness—one that is hardly conducive to open inquiry or the potental rewards of the creative process.

A more propitious attitude is to see ourselves not only as the subject of change but also as the agent of change for others. Engaging with others as their benefactor not only enables our companions to move more assuredly towards their particular goals, but also enables us to get on with our own

* Two titles that I recommend are *You and Me: The Skills of Communicating and Relating to Others* by Gerard Egan (Monterey, Calif.: Brooks/Cole Publishing Co., 1977) and *Messages; The Communication Book* by Matthew McKay, Martha Davis, and Patrick Fanning (Oakland, Calif.: New Harbinger Publications, 1983).

evolution. As we employ our resourses to further the growth of someone else, we become more beneficent, more expressive and expansive. In the act of helping others we are transformed in like manner.

Stopping the World

If we are challenged by things we already know, our responses will likely be well made, drawn as they are from our standing repertoire of skills and knowledge. But to what end? To exhibit what we already know? That's OK for kids, but transformation is bigger and better stuff. For these grander ambitions we require grander means, and again we can turn to the patterns of ritual for guidance.

When ritual is employed to fulfill transformative ambitions we notice that the novice is forced to confront challenges that stand outside of his or her usual range of experience. The challenge must be of such a magnitude that ordinary ways of being will not suffice. The invitation to engage in Creative Encounters must be made in such a manner as to "stop the world" so that a new world may be entered.

Creative Encounters are like this. In some essential ways they are designed to resemble Zen koans or Native American vision quests. Such confrontations are indeed unsettling, which is precisely what we wish *momentarily* to do: to unsettle established patterns so that new patterns may be created that account more completely for the actual grandeur of the world and our own possibilities. Creative Encounters need to be so designed as to make the challenge awesome (inspiring awe) and at the same time sufficiently inviting. We desire an engaging problem, one that is reflective, inward-seeking, and solvable, and that will require close scrutiny of all possibilities.

We can describe a typical encounter as follows. "In a guided imagery in which you travel ten years into the future, you meet two 'yous'; each one takes a different path to the future. One path is labeled "the probable path," the other, "the possible path." Having seen yourself as a result of following each of these two divergent paths for a decade, draw the person who is at the end of each one." The encounter with our possible and our probable self is meant to present us with an invitation to pause in the doing of our life and, as we stand back from it, to reflect upon its ultimate dimensions. The casting of the engagement ought to strike at a deep and central definition of self. In our example the issue is not simply how we will age physically (although how we do age physically is not a trivial matter); larger still is the issue of how we *define* ourselves as we age. How we conceive of ourselves is a more pivotal determinant of our quality of life than is our facade.

In other sections of this book I have spoken of core issues that should be addressed in the design of Creative Encounters. What makes us unique? What makes us universal? Where do we wish to go from here? How can we forgive when we can't forget? To the degree to which an encounter goes to the heart of the matter, to that same degree is the transformation of those key traits likely to occur.

We find this same concern for central features of the self at issue in transformative rituals. In matters of birth, marriage, fecundity, health, and status, rituals are the social vehicle whereby individuals and groups move to preferred situations. The fact that one must move on gives a sense of completion or fullness to the rites, a fullness that takes the form of introspection and expression. Just what we desire for our own Creative Encounters.

Solitude and Communion

Rituals are significantly communal affairs as well as individual enterprises. It is the one who is healed, but it takes the many to accomplish the act of healing. It is this dual nature of rituals that next concerns us. Each one of us is an island universe glowing with the hubbub of internal vitality. Our millions of cells, dozens of organs, rivers of fluid, and electrical systems mirror the beat and stuff of the rest of the universe. And we are components of a stupendous whole that stretches out infinitely in time and space. We are simultaneously both starkly alone and inextricable companions to all. Thus in our process of transformative encounters we do well to honor both dimensions of our being. The design of our encounters should have their own particular cadence of events, times for solitary work and times for communion. The times of solitude are opportunities for individual work as well as for private meditations. It is customary to provide adequate time to physically work on the "thing"; less honor is accorded to private reflections. As a result people can't help but be less reflective, and this is a great loss. We want to respect the life of the mind at all levels of awareness; we want to honor being as much as we recognize the importance of doing. Give time over for these private silences and quiet reflections. Nurture these qualities. The same qualities are essential components of the creative process.

Therefore—as is traditional in the vision quest of Native Americans—we need to design our encounters so as to provide time for retreating from the world of others so that we may plumb our inner dimensions undisturbed by the world as it is. And then we must provide time for reentering the world, sharing our discoveries, and having these same discoveries affirmed by our companions.

Different goals require the design of different rituals, each one emphasizing particular forms of transformation. Our whole ambition is to invigorate our powers of expressive imagination so that the world we make for ourselves is created from a wide palette of possibilities and so that as a consequence we may live in our own particular form of grace. The following portions of this chapter deal with the design of Creative Encounters intended to foster these goals.

RESPONDING FROM WITHIN

Earlier I said that the most important characteristic of the Creative Encounter is that the respondent must, for the answer, draw from within, at the sufficiently profound level of self-awareness where no ready answers reside. The question should "stop the world," require us to pause and stand back from the ordinary flow of our lives and reflect upon its underlying patterns and its ultimate possibilities.

What we encounter at this level is material that lies right at the center of that which makes us the people we are. Because these qualities lie so close to our behaviors and worldview, they appear to form the entire fabric of our world, causing their (our) boundaries to fade as they (we) stretch to the farthest reaches of our ken. It is difficult to find an "edge" to this overspreading fabric. To do so takes an encounter with a bite, requiring us to grasp, tug, and test the extent of what we have touched. We won't find our domain by seeking after external signs. What we seek is already there within us, but is not, on first assay, discernable. If the effort is honest and persistent, however, what we seek will be eventually uncovered. When we finally travel far from the ordinary and make every effort to transcend our own guile and impatience, our achievement will be to return home and see home (really ourselves) as if for the very first time. This is not an original observation, but it is true and terribly important for anyone who had cast his or her lot as an artist.

THE SUBJECT OF CREATIVE ENCOUNTERS

The subject content of creative encounters can be stated simply: it is the nature of the self. As our self comes to awareness as a result of contact with the world, thereby creating our life, creative encounters address those elements of our life that have significantly increased or expanded our sense of self and our place in the world. We are not interested here in marking time or in entertainments; we want to move on to our preferred life, past where we have come from and with increased impetus.

Questions dealing with pivotal people in our lives, for example, can provide the impetus for real engagement. Of all the people in your life, who was that person who made you feel "seen and worthy"? And if you were asked to create a visual monument to that person's memory, what would it look like, where would it be located? What metaphor can you create to embody the quality of his or her contribution to you? Similarly, questions dealing with key episodes of life provide a rich mine of themes. Such a question might be worded this way: We are all changed in some fashion by life's major events. What event of your life precipitated an *awakening?* What did you "know" about life before this event, and what did you know after? What was the "look of the feel" as you emerged from this old self into the new? Notice here the request to seek a pivotal moment in life and to portray not the image of the event itself, but the subjective experience of moving from one level of consciousness to a more elevated one. This creative endeavor affirms the transformative value of the event and thus encourages our availability for further such adventures of mind and spirit.

UNIVERSAL APPLICATION

Creative Encounters should invite the widest possible audience to respond with serious interest. It might seem at first that this criterion would lead to rather bland and shallow themes. It doesn't. These encounters not only go deep, but also have a universal appeal. Put another way, if the engagement does not strike a significant portion of the population as compelling, it is likely to be either obscurely couched or of minor, local interest. Later I will speak about clearly presenting the idea; here we will focus on the issue of pertinence.

For example, who would not be engaged by this question: "What quality about you is the irreducible element without which you would cease being the person you take yourself to be?" Notice that no particular creed, value system, social status, or experiential background precludes serious engagement with this question. Notice, too, that no special knowledge of the world is required here. No threshold of familiarity with a particular area of knowledge is imposed that would limit the significance of the question.

Furthermore, the question is presented in terms that are easily understood. The vocabulary may be modified for particular people in different settings, but essentially it is a straightforward question. Of course, a full response will not be a simple matter, but then this is precisely what we are after: depth, courage, imagination, verve. Note also how carefully the question is shaped to evoke real depth of interpretation, penetration, and expression.

For example, if instead of asking, "What quality about you . . . ," we asked, "What possession of yours . . . ," we would confine the response to the representation of things, eliminating the consideration of traits of mind, skills, emotions, and so on. Or, if instead of asking about "the irreducible element," we ask about the "best" element, or the most conspicuous, agreeable, or interesting element, we would have confined the range of possibilities to a predetermined set of choices that might not be as deep or crucial as those evoked by the attribute "irreducible."

Finally, suppose we asked, not, ". . . which you would cease being the person you take yourself to be," but instead, ". . . which others would recognize you as being you" or, "without which you could not carry on the life that you have." Interesting as these questions are, they do not invite the depth of inner investigation shown by the original question; rather, they ask that you focus your concerns on what other people think of you.

If we can constrict the range of responses by asking a confined question, we can also weaken the vigor of the response by phrasing the question so broadly as to invite safe or shallow responses. For example, if instead of asking about the "irreducible" quality, we asked about the "best qualities," we would be issuing an invitation to go not deep, but merely wide. Or if we asked for the elements that make us "special," we would be inviting a list of any number of traits with no hierarchy: an endless and not particularly penetrating task.

Some term in the question has to provoke depth, some term has to invite individual interpretation, some term has to set limits on the inquiry. In the question "What quality about you is the irreducible element without which you would cease being the person you take yourself to be?" "irreducible" is the term that provokes depth, "you take yourself to be" invites individual interpretation, and "without which you would cease to be" defines the limits of the inquiry.

NONRHETORICAL

In designing Creative Encounters, it is important that we are not led to a predetermined destination that is actually a projection of the questioner's own preferences. For instance, suppose we were interested in inquiring after the essential characteristics of our selves. What if, instead of saying, "Find that quality of you without which you would no longer be the person you take yourself as being," we said, "Find that quiet balanced point, at the very center of your being, from which your strength derives"? By including the phrase "quiet balanced point" we characterize a region and a quality that may not exactly fit the respondent's own inclinations. By being presented at the very outset of the quest, this phrase guides the respondent toward certain areas of inquiry and away from others. For instance, we may not experience our essential characteristic as having a particular location (the very center of your being); instead, it may be experienced as atmospheric, enveloping. If it does have a specifiable location, it may not be at the center but in a particular body region or region outside of the self. The attributes "quiet" and "balanced" may be equally misplaced. It may be quite tumultuous in there, a cool but eternal fire, a white noise, a maelstrom, a fountain.

If our question is too broadly worded, the respondent may fall back on safe and ordinary answers. Overly specific leading questions may attract the respondent to areas of only marginal concern to them. In either case we achieve responses that do little to advance the transformative process. We can better employ our time and energy in plunging down deeply, encountering the furniture of the psyche.

Rhetorical questions or questions that lead to particular, predetermined

ends are soon found out for what they are, a confinement of free will, a devious means of making a statement rather than asking a question, and ultimately they reveal a lack of real interest in the respondent. As a consequence, the respondent must eventually mistrust the questioner and the questions alike. I am reminded here of the classic comic line "Well, that's enough about me. Let's talk about you: What do you think about me?"

Inviting a person to set out on an uncertain journey inevitably creates some degree of anxiety. Who can tell what will be discovered? Who can tell how far from home the journey will take us? How will we ever find our way back again—and back to where? None of us will embark on such a journey without feeling that our mentor is fully trustworthy, has our best interests in mind, and will be there completely for us throughout the journey. So, no leading questions. Please.

DEPTH RATHER THAN CORRECTNESS

Creative Encounters are presented in such terms that the question may be penetrated past facile and unexamined work to truly genuine engagement with things of importance. Whatever the look of the work, what we seek to cultivate is fullness of engagement, rather than correctness of effort. And this puts the engagement in an entirely different category of goals and means.

As I noted before, efforts which can be measured by degrees of wrong and right must employ an external standard imported from a standing lexicon of "goodness." This lexicon originates in other minds, themselves the products of other times, places, and circumstances. In this way we are always being measured against someone else; as a result, all our efforts are competitive. What is more, we do battle with adversaries with whom actual engagement is impossible since they are no longer present, even though it is upon their terms and standards that we will be judged!

Not only is virtually every personal act thus set within a context of fierce competition, but the competition is so structured as to be unwinnable. The only way to extricate ourselves from this sort of right-wrong engagement is to deconstruct the competition as given and create our own rules, goals, and standards. This is what every original person does in a myriad of small ways. It is also what the great heroic figures of originality do in vast ways. In our time, Freud, Marx, Einstein, Picasso, Joyce, Stravinsky all smashed through the conceptual frameworks of good and bad, wrong and right that society presented to them and created their own visions and vocabularies out of the need to be judged in terms of their own intentions rather than by older, inapplicable standards. Gilgamesh, Siddhartha, Moses, Jesus, and Muhammad did likewise.

In removing us from the context of competition, Creative Encounters place us within a rarefied domain. In this space, with no external signs to guide the way or measure the catch, how can we know the value of our findings? How can we know how deep and thorough our engagement is? I think there are two systems of measurement at work here. The first is internal and private, the second public and reactive. Our bodies are made to register the subtlest degrees of pleasure and discomfort, anxiety and well-being. Every one of our billions of cells is quite alive and in constant vigilance over the very smallest shifts in its viability. A few more ions of sodium or potassium in a cell throw the place into a riot of urgent pleas to the rest of the universe of cells through hundreds of miles of neural wiring, to get those damn ions out of there *now*. We really are constructed rather well. We may not know what's happening to the point of speaking descriptively of what is happening, no less why, nor to what ends, but our wiring is very nicely made and our biological stuff does a good job of "knowing" what's going on and *expressing* what is happening rather well. If we turn our conscious attention to monitor what our body is *already* expressing, we will be provided with revealing information concerning how it's going out there/in here.

Where we are allowing our brush free play and we are presented with deeply new visual material, how can we know how deep we went when no one has been there before to leave us a depth chart? We know how deep we are because our ears pop, our eyes feel pushed in, our chest gets squashed, our cheeks cave in, our temples ring, our fingers tingle, our temperature drops. *Where* we are is determined by *how we feel* about where we currently are. What we know of where we are is a description of how we are experiencing being alive where we are. We know when we haven't gone far enough because we'll feel that there is a reservoir of untested strength, endurance, skills, and knowledge still in reserve. We'll feel flat, missing something, not necessarily knowing the identity or the quantity of what is not sufficiently there, but definitely being aware that we are not sated.

Knowing when we have arrived is known in a similar manner. Everything may be new, but familiar nonetheless in a sure if nonspecifiable way. We feel well, things fit, there's an uncrowded feeling, we are unhurried. Breathing is full and unencumbered, our limbs move easily in unself-conscious ways. We take cognizance of our situation as lovers do of one another. Every texture, ripple, color, and aroma is entirely new and is carefully mapped. Our mind acknowledges by a hundred different signs what our body is flashing: *This is it!* or *This is not it!* In this way we "know" the fullness and accuracy of our response. The *meaning* of that response may not be clear at all at first. Nothing newly emerged presents its all, all at once. Study, proximity, patience, maturing, care, slowly build an increasingly sensitive interface between the thing out there and the thing within.

BEYOND MEMORY AND ILLUSTRATION

Memory is not easy to retrieve, either in its fullness or in its actual details. We think we have the past in mind, but on closer examination it often turns out to be terribly out of focus and missing major components. When we attempt to describe what we believe we remember, the portrayal we offer frequently disappoints; it is flatter, paler, softer than what actually occurred. Or we so exaggerate the case, that what we say no longer resembles what we experienced. An exact memory, able to dump the past into the present without spilling anything, is a powerful attribute of mind that few people have. The endless social gossip that we think of as remembering past events is really not much more than blab as entertainment.

Who, What, Where, When, and How? These questions provoke memory to loosen its hold. Much is actually there, and a huge inventory of memories may be accessed, selected from, and drawn forward in response. Material that is honest, thoughtful, and eventually well-crafted comes from such use of the mind. If practiced in fullness, art generated from such a condition can be rewarding for the artist and certainly for the viewer. Our memories contain our entire grasp of our lives. Memory—if indeed it is memory and not fantasy—can be a rational stock-taking of the inventory of the events of our past, or a grand act of the mind that allows the ephemera of private lives to enter the public domain of history. Pivotal events that sculpted our personal identities, our values, our very naming and locating ourselves in the world all reside in our memories. And as has been said so often, memory also allows us to convey the lessons derived from one generation to the next and thereby avoid (so they say) the costs incurred the first time around.

We could spend our days as artists giving physical presence to what is already contained in our memories, already a picture in our mind's eye. But wouldn't this be making the present a slave to the past? Wouldn't this employ our genius only to illustrate what has hitherto been our fate?

Much intelligence derives from conscious acts of mind such as memory, but not all thought is generated at the conscious level. There is thoughtfulness above and below the conscious strata: for instance dreaming. Acts of imagination, daydreaming, fantasies, visions, much gesture and utterance, all derive from the subconscious, intuitive levels rather than the level of conscious recall.

We would like to pose our Creative Encounters in such a fashion as to engage both kinds of intelligence. We seek to engage the subconscious domain of mind for the same reasons that psychologists, shamans, and lovers do: there is a unique richness and quality here that determine significant portions of our life. This dimension contains resources and powers not held at the conscious level. As Rollo May points out, speaking of the contributions of the subconscious not only to the arts but to the sciences,

> creativity coming from the preconscious and unconscious is not only important for art and poetry and music; but is essential in the long run also for our science. To shrink from the anxiety this entails, and block off the threatening new insights and forms this engenders, is not only to render our society banal and progressively more empty, but also to cut off as well the headwaters in the rough and rocky mountains of the stream that later becomes the river of creativity in our science.[27]

We know with some degree of effectiveness how to induce the conscious mind to solve a given problem by performing a very elaborate series of intellectual feats, and most of us do this rather well. (What is not of small interest here, most of us execute these steps subconsciously, or at least below the level of awareness.) For example, the question "What one trait about yourself do you hold most dear?" requires an extremely complex series of deliberations, without the respondent's needing to have the vaguest idea how these deliberations were carried out. The same is true for carrying on most conversations, however intricate or banal they may be.

We also know various ways to gain access to the subconscious or subliminal mind. Psychologists have devised such techniques as hypnotic states, rapid word associations, guided imagery, and the like. Shamans and clerics have other methods: chanting, fasting, dancing, psychotropic materials, and so on. Lovers have still other ways. The creative process is yet another means by which the resources of the subconscious may be tapped. The creative process incorporates elements of these other methods, but sets them within a configuration particular to itself. The subject of creativity is a vast area of study, and it is not my intention to cover it here. Let me simply add to my earlier remarks that the creative process is, to a significant degree, a somatic act, one in which the physical body expresses what is known in those portions of the brain that operate nonverbally and that rely upon image and gesture to convey their knowledge.

The mind's conscious, verbalizing dimension can make contact with the subconscious dimension when it cognizes the signing that is flashed, in code form, by the somatically articulate brain. Creative people, whatever else they know, also know how to connect with the signs being sent by the subconscious mind in the form of sound, image, or gesture, and they know how to accurately relay those signs into coherent expression.

As Freud discovered, and as Jung, Rank, and later Rollo May elaborated and refined, when the conscious and the subconscious became acquainted with each other, a new persona is born. A whole, awake, compassionate person steps forward from the one who was previously fractured, incomplete, and at war within himself or herself. Those early analysts observed, as do therapists in general, a sudden burst of enthusiasm for living in such cases, a quickening of the senses, an acceptance of the self as it is and the world as it is. As an outcome of this meeting of the minds, this reconciliation, there is an inexorable blossoming of creativity.

That is what we desire. That is why we must provide opportunities that engage the participant at both levels of mind.

We know we are addressing the resources of the subconscious mind when we begin to make things (sounds, images, gestures) *without* knowing what we are doing or what it may mean. The uninitiated dismiss this activity as meaningless—and unfortunately, they are in part correct, it *is* meaningless. But they fail to understand that this is a necessary phase of a much more elaborate series of mental operations that do eventuate in meaning. Misapprehending the activity as a complete act, they never proceed along to the next phases and accordingly never gain, indeed never could gain, the

97

rewards. Those who know otherwise are our artists. They allow this phase (which may look from the outside like play or babble) to run its course for as long as possible. They know that the moment of judgment is all too soon upon them and that this subliminal material will then cease to flow in that moment. So they let their hand have its day. If we are determined, and manage to stay in the intuitive mode for a substantial period of time, we will accumulate many new perceptions. Later, at our leisure, we can cull the babble from the core message, refine it still further, and in so doing enrich ourselves and thus our art.

FEELINGS

Feelings: what a maudlin, hack word. What a mess of sloppy behavior and muddled thinking here. Yet how is one to account for the human experience if one expurgates feelings from consideration? We can substitute other, more elegant words for this adolescent-sounding term, *feelings.* One could instead speak of inclinations, sensibilities, impressions, susceptibilities, sensations, perceptions, sympathies. But I like the nasty little word, because it refers to a significant dimension of mind. The body literally *does* feel different, palpably different, in different emotional states. This connection between states of mind and body is most important for our thesis that the hand guides the eye and eventually guides the mind in the creation of transformative images.

Although every act of mind is accompanied by parallel emotions and physiological states, particular events provoke heightened emotional and physical reactions. Here we want to investigate how provocative events can be employed to enhance the creative process and the process of personal transformation. Events that strike us to the quick do so in a holistic manner; that is, whatever the single point of initial entry into our realm of awareness, intellect, emotion, or physical body, the resonance is experienced in all dimensions of our being. Things that really matter to any one dimension of our self matter to all. And the converse is equally true: mosquito bites may be annoying, but they are a surface and passing bodily impression, and as a consequence we rarely get excited about them intellectually, emotionally, or spiritually. A bop on the nose (or the soul) is another matter. Creative Encounters require provocations that set not only our body to swatting and jumping, but our souls. For that we need to invite Creative Encounters that do provoke us to reflect upon the meanings—not simply the data—of our lives.

To continue with my point about the wholistic character of our being, we are constructed in such a way that all our parts and all our traits are interconnected at the most profound level of intricacy. This is our nature. This is probably the nature of nature. There is an inherent reciprocity among our dimensions. Poke our system in at any one point, and it pops out in another place, not only once and in one place, but over and over again in many echoing reverberations. If we train ourselves to become cognizant of what our bodies already know and are expressing, we will have important and

accurate information that can guide us along our way. Any event will set us
to reacting, but some events (or questions, in this case) call us to greater
things than others do. What interests us is the way the entire self vibrates to
any single event, because we intend to utilize this phenomenon to nurture
and extend the creative process, and because this same creative process, art,
can be understood as the externalization of interior states of mind and body.

Big events set up big reverberations—big not only in scale, but in depth,
complexity, and subtlety. If we desire art that has great depth, complexity,
and subtlety (and we do), then we will do well to initiate its creation through
the design of major Creative Encounters that in turn precipitate deep feelings. Big feelings touch upon significant episodes of our life and touch those
memories at a great number of points, so that we reexperience the original
and now layered episode with substantial fullness. This can provide very
rich material for the creative process, while at the same time it makes available large amounts of expressive energies. It sets the mind-body-spirit to
vibrating sympathetically and heightens acuity in these same dimensions.
We can then channel this animated, synchronized, altered self in an ener-
gized state into creative endeavors.

There is often a fear that creative expressions made while under the influ-
ence of charged emotionality will feel better than they look. There is also
alarm that without the deliberations of a dispassionate mind, such efforts
may well be cathartic but lack the crafting that only cooler minds can exercise. In fact, in most cases this is true. I am not claiming that these natural
expressions are sufficient for the end results of the creative process, but I do
believe that they are essential for the initial foundation upon which authentic creative endeavors originate.

Once the experience eventuates in the work—that is, once the internal
event becomes externalized in the creation of metaphoric objects—we may
return to that primary effort, and if it is not sufficiently full and clear in its
expression then we may more deliberately refine it until it is. Craft is not
opposed to creative expression, it is the means by which private experience
becomes the object of public empathies. In some cases the initial expression exactly represents the internal state of affairs. In those cases leave it
alone; craft applied here will only lead to ornament. But if your intentions
exceed your execution, then work on.

SEQUENCING

Every intrepid traveler knows that each journey, no matter what its length
or degree of difficulty, begins with a single step. How one takes that initial
step and in what direction determines much of what will follow. As the

order of the journey unfolds, we need to design the sequence of our encounters while being mindful of several characteristics of journeys that seek not simply the new, but the transformative.

The invitation to take the first steps should be presented in such a way that everyone can take that step; in other words, it should present the lowest threshold to participation. If we feel in any way inadequate in these initial engagements, our sense of inadequacy is likely to permeate reactions to all subsequent activities. The initial engagement should therefore require the least amount of specialized information about art or any external subject matter. For instance, the following would seem a poor initial question: "If you could be any artist during the Italian Renaissance, who would you be and what would you paint?" A thoughtful introspective question, but one that presupposes detailed information about time, place, circumstance, style, and biographical information. No affect is required; it is all conscious and deliberate work. There is nothing personal to wrestle with and overcome. Furthermore, response to the question requires a degree of visual literacy and memory that not many people possess. A better phrasing might be: "If you could transport yourself to any time and any place, where would you go, when would you arrive, and what would you see?" Here, the respondent can go to any time and any place, and the only place they can go is where they *can* go; the place is of *their* choice and making, not the questioner's. They can image whatever they are capable of imaging, not something esoteric and difficult as is the task of imaging someone else's style of seeing and image making.

The first steps ought to be technically easy for the same reasons. Technique is always one of the great fears of any apprentice. The greater the fear, the greater the preoccupation with technical things. This in turn leads to timidity about the scope of imagination, narrowness of range of expression, and a concern for safety rather than depth. Suppose we wish to explore issues relative to the qualities of life that move us in some substantial ways. In engaging this issue, we want to feel comfortable with those skills we presently have, to feel that they are sufficient for the task at hand. A formulation that would raise the technical threshold unacceptably high might sound like this: "Peonies have long been an ancient Eastern symbol of eternal affection. Choose a type of peony that speaks best of your affection for a loved one and render it with parallel love." The problem is a reflective one and requires both thoughtfulness and feeling, but the technical knowledge demanded (to be able to choose from and render several types of peonies!) is substantial. A more effective phrasing demanding minor technical difficulty might be: "If you could symbolize the person you love in the form of a flower, what would that real or imaginary flower look like?" Inviting consideration of *any* flower rather than a *specific* flower (especially one as complex as the peony) allows us to visualize what we *can* visualize. And inviting the use of an image based upon what we ourselves have seen or imagined allows those of us whose visual imagination is superior to our visual memory to respond fully with our own particular intellectual style and degree of technical facility.

The invitation to take the initial step must also be offered in such a manner that the emotional depth or height is acceptable. No one ought to be urged to reveal intimacies or search out vulnerabilities in the company of new companions. The degree of companionship is still to be tested, trust still to be won, confidence yet to be established. Only through a gradual evolution of sharing and mutual support is an atmosphere of trust developed. Therefore the initial invitation to engagement ought to be presented in such a fashion that all participants will feel comfortable with expressing—and thus exposing—what they deem proper to their own sense of dignity and privacy.

An example of a question that is too intrusive for an initial encounter might be this: "What is the look and feel of the fears that keep you from being the person you prefer to be?" This question penetrates to our very heart. It is extremely evocative and thus rich in its potential for authentic creative engagement. However, no one should be called to that door of inquiry who has not first been surrounded by a tested community of supportive peers. For once elicited, the material contained in the response *must* work its way out in expressed ideas, emotions, and behaviors. There must be a reciprocating community, or at least a partner, who is able and willing to be there for us as we subsequently grapple with this potentially transformative material.

A phrasing of the encounter that invites depth but without any compulsion to do so might be: "We all can imagine ourselves in a preferred state of being somewhat in advance of the person we currently take ourselves as being. Reflect on that preferred you—more on the feel than the look of it—and discover ways of representing that feel of the desired you." The focus here is more on the reflective claiming and defining of a self and less upon the location of an historical hurt, or a sorrow or fear. The effort is still reflective, personal, deep, and significant but does not require the sharing of intimacies, painful or otherwise, before there are trustworthy intimates with whom to share them.

The initial portions of the creative journey have as their prime purpose the establishment of a sense of trust and comfort in oneself, one's peers, and the general kind of terrain to be explored. Once this foundation is developed, we can move on to the subsequent phase of the transformative journey, a gradual expansion of the invitation to fathom the whole depth and range of our thoughts and feelings concerning the place in the world we would have for ourselves.

This central phase of the creative journey seeks out deeper, often more profound levels of mind, emotion, and spirit. Here we are dealing with more sensitive dimensions of our self-consciousness; therefore we must create an even more supportive atmosphere where we may feel more confident in employing the powers of our intuitive mind. This same context allows for larger periods of judgment-free creative play and the exercise of ever increasing skill at being a supportive mentor to others while being the same for ourself. During this period, trust grows proportionally to expressed creativity. Or perhaps it may be more accurate to say that creative expression can expand only as far and as rapidly as trust expands.

Trust is such an overused word that it is important here to specify its meaning and power. *Webster's Unabridged Dictionary* has a nice way of presenting both its meaning as a word and its meaning in our lives. The definition goes like this."*Trust:* a confidence, a reliance or resting of the mind on the integrity, veracity, justice . . . of another person or thing." It's this "resting of the mind" that I want to call attention to. For in the mind's rest waits the intuitive, subliminal, subconscious activity of the mind. While there is no trust, the conscious mind will never allow its subconscious counterpart to hold sway. So engendering ever greater degrees of trust is not simply to create a pleasant working atmosphere. Creating an atmosphere within which trust is engendered permits the scope of imagination to be extended, increases our range of risk-taking, and allows material from our subconscious to find expression unimpeded by the gates of our judgment-prone conscious mind.

Trust builds upon the favorable outcome of preceding events. Trust builds not arithmetically, but exponentially. And it is destroyed in the same way. Thus we want to design and arrange the order of our encounters in such a manner so as to take advantage of the exponential growth and collapse of trust. Each encounter ought to be shaped not simply to fit but, even more, to extend the growing edge of the region of trust as it is enlarged by experience. I have called this kind of planning "sequencing," a concept illustrated by the following series of creative encounters. (The encounters themselves are described in detail in chapter 4.)

1. *Going to the Infinite Well.* Find any object that somehow is metaphorically descriptive of you, and make sixty one-minute variations of that object, using any medium of your choice (pencil, charcoal, paints, etc.). Next, take one of the sixty most engaging to you and in six five-minute works extend that image further down the road of your imagination each

time. Finally, take one of these six variations—the one most pregnant with further possibilities—and take it wherever it wants to go. (See pages 124–127 for details.)

2. *The Nub of You:* Reflect upon that quality of yourself without which you would no longer be the person you take yourself to be. Explore what that quality may be like, in the creation of a work named for that quality. (See pages 149–151.)

3. *Janus Masks.* We each have a public and a private face or persona: one we show to acquaintances and associates, while the other is reserved only for intimates. Create a mask representing the look and feel of each, then, facing a partner who puts on first your public, then your private mask, speak to each mask in turn, saying what needs to be said to each, speaking aloud of the rewards of, and the price paid for, wearing each one. (See pages 152–156.)

"Going to the Infinite Well" is essentially a boundary-breaking encounter exercising the limits of imagination. It is alternately exhilarating and fatiguing, but there is little at risk here. "The Nub of You" asks you to be more reflective, more interior, invites you to look deep inside to your source of strength and being. The journey is more personal than the first, and more celebratory once completed. "Janus Masks" is more reflective still, touches directly upon inner conflicts and invites their direct confrontation. It requires more interaction between the conscious and subconscious minds, between the public and the private self, and between the self and another human being. In this way there is a greater region of dynamic tension involved and thus more to be wrestled with (and hopefully to be resolved). Each one adds another dimension of our self to the encounter, as each additional dimension moves deeper to more significant and vulnerable domains. Each one further tests our mettle, increasing the arena of necessary risk and consequently the potentiality of reward.

TIMING

We swim in time; it is the medium of our living. Duration alone creates heroes and cowards, victory and defeat. The same embrace held a moment too briefly is a sign of flagging affections; held a mite too long, it becomes an act of quiet desperation. Creative Encounters also exist within an exact time frame. The need to consider and create a self-portrait within ten minutes gives rise to a different set of encounters, thoughts, and images than the same assignment with an allotment of two hours or two days or two months or two years or two minutes. A brief journey allows for certain things, longer durations encourage others. A short journey is like a short tether: you can't get very far from home. But sometimes that's nice, you can't stray far from home and you know it, so you can indulge in antics that you probably wouldn't consider if you had a longer tether or no tether at all. It's scary out there; it's safe close to home. You act differently when you are scared than when you feel safe.

Short-term engagements invite spontaneity, playfulness and risk-taking of a kind. Quick, ten-second works promote expressive gestures and cultivate raw utterances rather than crafted eloquence, admittedly at the risk of shallowness and carelessness. Lengthy time periods promote thorough searching and deep penetration of complex grounds. With adequate time you can afford to dawdle, saunter about, observe minutely all that catches your attention. The danger here is that large amounts of time may heighten self-consciousness to a paralyzing degree. When imagination has run its course and there is still much time to fill, the work may become tedious. We kill time and our work by tidying it up, nice and neat and dead.

Each person and each group has a unique rhythm to bring to the journey, and that rhythm evolves based upon what has just occurred and what is foreseeable. Therefore no hard formulas can be offered as to effective time periods for each encounter and their pacing. Nevertheless, we can be aware that timing does matter, that the envelope of time within which any creative activity takes place will be a major determinant of the depth and breadth of that engagement.

APPROACHING CLOSURE

At some point the journey will end. Our companions on this journey will go their separate ways, and the group will disperse. We will move on to other directions and means of awakening. Concluding hard-won and uniquely rewarding associations is not a simple matter and certainly not an inconsequential one. This section speaks of endings and commencements.

The transformative journey through the creative process acquaints us with heights and depths that we are not likely to encounter during the normal course of our lives. There have been revelations, successful risk-taking, mutual support, and the realized goal of our particular ambition: substantial growth in zeal and capacity for creative enterprises. We are not the same individuals who began this journey. We have experienced ways of being and thinking and feeling and communing that we may not have experienced before. The community of others within which we have labored has created a supportive envelope to protect and nurture this expansion. It has been a good and most likely a rare time. And now it is time to move on once again.

If our journey has made us aware of anything about the creative process, surely it is the inexorable requirement of being awakened to ever-widening planes of consciousness. We are born once biologically, but we may be born many times intellectually and spiritually. Each time we do, we must give up one level of awareness and succeed to the next. And as we all know, growth is not a simple act of acceding to the new; it is also saying farewell to the old, much of which has been dearly acquired and with which our hearts and minds in large measure are still engaged. Gaining the new must be paralleled with relinquishing our hold on the past. We must find new ways to love and think about the past. And we must create new ways to become acquainted with and learn to love the open territory that as of yet has no name, only promise. As we enter into this concluding/commencing phase, we need to design encounters that help us to relinquish our hold on the past and to prepare ourselves to enter a new, more promising landscape

Elisabeth Kübler-Ross has observed that among the terminally ill patients she has worked with, the ones who have the most difficulty accepting their imminent death are those who feel they have left unsaid and undone things of the heart and of spirit. Not that they didn't get a chance to build big and high enough, but that they didn't get to say "I love you" and "Thank you" to the people who really mattered in their lives. This time of moving on is a good time to say "I love you" to all the people who have been there for us during our journey, to all the things of the world which touched us and helped us awaken. This is a time to say "Thank you" for all the gifts that have come our way, bidden and unbidden, those that were sought after and particularly those that just flopped into our laps, like starlight, springtime, eyesight, mind, dreams, the ability to feel love, its presence and absence. This is a time for reflecting upon and affirming the presence of the indestructable inner core of our being, which goes with us wherever desire, chance, and destiny have us go.

The design of a Creative Encounter that concludes a series should contain elements of reflection on what gifts have come about as a consequence of the work done during this period and/or been revealed by the process. And there ought to be ways designed to overtly declare our gratitude for those gifts. The encounter "Random Acts of Kindness, Senseless Gifts of Beauty" on pages 162–164 is an example of this process.

CLOSURE

Creative Encounters bring about many—sometimes large—dislocations of the mind and spirit. The person who enters this arena of creative growth is not the person who emerges. We have to be ready to meet this sometimes tender, sometimes exuberantly bold, but in any event certainly new self. Once one process has proceeded through the active phases of discovering a grander self, it is time for reflection. And this too must be accommodated in the design of the series.

This is a time for private synthesis and public affirmation. To speak of the need for privacy first. During the course of these Creative Encounters you have most probably evolved more rapidly and are now somewhat out of sync with the world you knew. It is appropriate then to have some time and space to be alone with your thoughts in order to become acquainted with how the world now looks and feels. While you review these experiences, a quiet walk by yourself for a while, silent meditation, or even a period of lazily crafting an earlier creative enterprise will offer you the opportunity to begin to synthesize the newly emergent features of the world with those more familiar. The stroking of immediate memory tends to confirm the actuality of our achievements and often teases out from the complexity of the original experience further qualities that may have been initially hidden or too subtle to emerge from the background of active give and take.

I have said several times that although we are born and live out our singular life and die alone, we do all this in the intimate and necessary company of others. When we have just completed a cycle of change due to our transformative journey through the creative process, some degree of dislocation between the people who matter in our life and ourselves is likely to develop. The companions with whom you took this journey matter and are a ready source of affirmation of the emergent in you. Often our companions will notice qualities about us that we will not see because these qualities are so new, so subtle, or so close. There may be, for instance, a more open posture, a deeper, calmer voice, a greater degree of warmth and animation in appearance, more expression in our face and gestures. And these same signs of heightened vitality may also appear in our work: richer blends of colors, a wider variety of marks, compositions that subsume the parts more completely, deeper rhythmic structures, clarity in expression, daring in things of the imagination. More than likely, these important signs of the distance we have traveled will be noticed first by others.

An example of such an exchange coming at the close of working together might be the following.

Anne: There was a moment during this week when I felt particularly anxious, and it's an old and silly thing, but I feel it all the time anyway. It's whenever I'm asked to choose a partner to work together as we were asked to in "Visual Dialogues." At these times I always feel so frightened that nobody will pick me, or that if I pick someone they won't want to work with me. I know this is kindergarten stuff, but it just gets to me. Well, this time when we were asked to find someone to work with, instead of that old and usual fear, I had an immediate image in mind. It was, I want to work with Linda. She had used the color orange in ways that I had never seen before. It was so delicious! I wanted to have some of that wonderful way with color for myself. So I knew who I had to work with and this was the first opportunity, so—*bam!*

Linda: You did? You really wanted to work with me? I did what with color?

Anne: Oh yes, ever since you worked with those oranges I had my eye on you, watching how you did things.

Linda: How *I* did things? What things? I'm a little embarrassed by this.

Anne: Well, you just plunged in with those soft, creamy pale oranges first. They seemed colors that I wouldn't dare to use, they were too—oh, too—scrumptious, like you should eat them, not see them.

Linda: Anne, really, eat them?

Anne: Well, that's the way I felt. Then you interestingly added some strokes of cool blue and pale greens into it, which made the thing start to shimmer in a way. I said to myself, I want that, I want to make my stuff alive like she does.

Linda: But Anne, it's just the way I do things, it's just, well, something I do.

Anne: But it is special. No one else here works color like you do, Linda, and for me it's very exciting how inventive you are, how outrageous you

109

allow yourself to be in your combinations of colors. They don't lead to a jumble of bashing colors, but rather make the surface just glisten and pulsate. Well, then you added on top of that earlier stuff hotter oranges. That added a third layer of warmth, and the thing just swam.

Linda: It did? It does?

Anne: It does, and so when I went directly up to you and asked if you would be my partner, and you smiled so simply and said yes, I wanted to laugh and I felt like crying with relief.

Linda: And when you so quickly came right up to me and asked if we could be partners, I felt, oh my, someone wants to work with me! How bold she is, I wish I had her assertiveness and confidence! I want to work with this person. I want to learn from her!

Anne: Oh, Linda, thank you. That's wonderful.

Linda: Thank you, Anne. I'm so glad we bumped into each other.

Sharing may be done in pairs or small subgroups or among all present at once. Obviously, the degree of intimacy, vulnerability, risk taking, and magnitude of affirmation will vary with the setting. As always, being sensitive to the emotional climate and the apparent needs of the group as a dynamic whole will determine which format of exchange is most effective.

Sharing these observations often brings to attention qualities that we may not have dared to notice or acknowledge. This is a time for solid companionship, for telling one another with care what we see and what we feel and listening with undivided attention. This is not the time for strenuous attempts to help the other with clarifying questions, clever observations, or conspicuous sympathies. Rather it is a time for taking full acount of what is currently seen or felt by both parties. It may also be a time for shared silences. The need during this concluding phase of the Creative Encounter is to be seen by someone else for the new person we are and, in the mirror of our companion's perceptions of ourself, affirm that indeed we are new.

4

Twelve Creative Encounters

INTRODUCTION

This chapter offers twelve examples of creative encounters. They are presented with the intention of illustrating what our general philosophy looks like in actual practice. These illustrations embody the principles of designing Creative Encounters as described in the previous chapter. Each encounter has been designed with a certain population in mind: adults of all ages who have a wide range of prior art training, from all-but-none to extensive, and whose commitment to the creative act ranges from that of the serious amateur to that of the veteran professional. Skill and technical proficiency ranges from modest in the extreme to advanced. While this range is extensive, it is not all-inclusive. For people outside of this population, that is, those who are younger or much older, or people with exceptional physical, intellectual, or emotional needs and resources, encounters can be modified to fit their particular situations.

The time required for these encounters varies in practice from one hour to three hours at a stretch. If your working context allows for time extending beyond these parameters, the designs may be modified accordingly. The frequency of the encounters will also be a consideration. I have conducted workshops lasting twelve hours a day for five days at a stretch. I have also conducted weekly three-hour sessions held over a period of six months as well as long-weekend studios. Whatever the arrangement, the encounters have a cumulative effect over time. Single experiences are more entertainments than anything else. By contrast, long-term practice of these exercises, like any long-term practice, brings a kind of inner rhythm and stability that affirms earlier growth and builds confidence for future and more ambitious engagements.

I stated earlier that these encounters can be profitable even if experienced alone: many of them, however, realize their fullest potential if carried out in the company of others. Working alone, working with another partner, or working in the company of greater numbers of participants will shift the dynamics of these (or any) experiences. Therefore feel free to modify these examples to suit your own circumstances. Encounters such as these, held in a supportive, nonjudgmental environment where the primary goal is clearly to further personal transformation through the creative act, have every prospect of achieving our basic goal: to move from an inherited to a chosen, intentional state of being.

Each encounter begins with setting the general context and the particular aspect of creative growth intended to be cultivated. This is followed by a step-by-step description of the process itself, which leads to the creation of an expressive image—the work of art. Each section concludes with a discussion of verbally processing the whole of the Creative Encounter, procedure and products, to elicit and shape the learnings that may have evolved.

METAPHORIC OBJECTS

Each one of us has several salient characteristics, the constellation of which comprises the being we take ourselves to be.

I, for instance, think of myself as having the following traits:

- An absolute fascination for the intricacy and fittedness of all living things
- A deep requirement for time by myself
- A love for sleep and the dream visions sleep invites
- A certain shyness acquired in early childhood that I'm reluctant to discard
- My full love of being a father to my son and daughter
- A love of big breakfasts
- A sense of revulsion at being confined, especially by small-minded people
- An enjoyment of slowness: movies that never end, walks that take all day, big fat juicy books, long winter naps, long summer evenings on the salt marshes fishing from my canoe, clumps of uninterrupted painting time in my studio, slow looking at what I have just painted

These and about a zillion other traits make me *me.*

But these traits are not just a hodgepodge of stuff crammed into the sack of my skin. They are arranged in a certain way, fluctuating to be sure from time to time, setting my complexion for that day. In my own special manner I stack and space these traits within the constellation that I call *myself.* How I arrange my components makes me hum in my own special way. Which element I give prominence to, which I take lightly, which elements I juxtapose, all create the unique form and pattern of my life.

I need space between my elements. Too tightly packed and I feel suffocated, too distant from one another and I feel disoriented. I also like syncopation in my life; regular intervals are foreign to me and make me feel confined and predictable. Geometric formations are inhospitable to my loose, improvisational spirit. Playful, airy, colorful, yet subtly centered is the way I like to think of myself. I'm more willow than oak, more forest than plain, more Brahms than Bach.

Not only are we composed of selections of things and arrangements thereof, we also exist in the larger context of place. *Where* we place ourselves in life is as telling as *what* gets placed. Some folks are, for the most part, center stage, some feel surer nearer to corners. Some feel good indoors, in soft, sinking-into spaces, others need wind and sunlight and tall skies. Some need a sheltered quiet cove of a space, others a broad and expansive plane. Still others feel best in high places, others in valleys and creases. I like to be near the cusp of things, not right on the edge, mind you, but nearby. The center holds too much hubris for me, the corners too much humility. I need light, air, room to move and to see far distances. But the sand flats of Florida and the limitless horizons of Oklahoma are too uninterrupted for this New Englander, used as he is to a variegated landscape.

Encounter

The objective of the following exercise is to explore these three main ingredients of self: What is salient about the self, how we compose those things into a personal constellation, and, finally, where in the world we locate ourself to best advantage.

Phase 1. Of all the things you are, of all the personality traits that make you essentially you, think of about half a dozen that come to your attention now, when the invitation to do so is offered. With these thoughts in mind, wander about wherever you happen to be for about a half an hour, watching for objects that strike you as somehow representative of these salient traits. It is not necessary to have an object in mind as you set out to find these metaphoric objects. In fact, if you do you will search with a kind of desperation, for the chance that you will come upon an object that resembles your mind-picture is all but nil. Rather just wander, saunter, allowing your eye to glide over the slowly passing landscape.

Remarkably—really, it never ever fails—the appropriate objects just seem to appear. Things you might not have thought of as being able to represent your personal traits will take on that metaphoric expressiveness if you look upon them in this frame of mind. After a short while, you may even experience the world coming to you, rather than you hunting after it. The world then seems studded with poignant symbols, rather than being a world dumb and devoid of meaning.

Having selected a half dozen or so metaphoric objects, it is now time to seek a place for them (you). Once again, rather than having a distinct image in your mind as to where these objects should be sited (sighted?), just wander around again, this time being sensitive to the varying degrees of well-being that may permeate your body as you move from place to place. Be aware of your bodily sensations as you orient yourself to different compass directions. Notice, too, your reactions to different degrees of light, different amounts of space between you and other things: walls, trees, windowsills, bushes, stairways, paths. And pay attention to your body as it reacts to the immediate colors, textures, smells, and sounds of this place and that. At some point in your wanderings, a certain place will feel just right, you will somehow feel: this is it. Don't worry that the reasons for this are obscure; your body knows, and your mind will eventually find its own way to account for and express the choices already being acknowledged by your body.

Phase 2. Having selected your metaphoric objects and located your special space, turn your attention now to composing those objects within that space. How to arrange the objects? Don't make art, don't be cute or clever. Just keep moving the stuff around until you feel it's OK. (You know what OK feels like: you breathe easily, your muscles are relaxed, your senses sharpen, you feel potent, safe, eager, OK.) That's it. No big deal, no searching, tearing your soul for just the correct composition. When you feel OK, it will be because you will experience a correspondence between how the outside of things look and how the inside of you feels. That's what we are doing here: finding ways to naturally express in and to the world what is happening to us within. And this is what art is about: creating physical metaphors to represent events of the mind.

Phase 3. The objects have been selected, the place found, the arrangement made. But the transformative potential of the experience is still to be derived. Most of what your hand and eye has been motivated to do so far has been done at a subliminal level of intelligence. Not that there has been no conscious intellect at work here, but a substantial number of the myriad choices you have been making have occurred at the subliminal level and have not derived from predetermined deliberate decisions. It is time for the rational dimension of your intellect to become acquainted with the intuitive wisdom that has guided you so far.

It will be of great help here to enlist the perceptions of others, for often we are wonderfully blind to the meanings which reside in our own intuitive utterances. Working, then, with one or more others who have also engaged in this project, the creator of each piece acts as host to the rest of the group, acquainting the group with the meanings intended by his or her choice of objects, the setting, and how they are composed within that setting. No truly original work makes the intentions of the artist explicit and clear either to the audience or to the artist. Therefore, this is a fruitful opportunity for both artist and companions to come to discover the meanings residing within the work.

You have located your work in a special setting, and it is important for you to set the conditions under which the rest of the group can gain access to your work and the meanings you have embedded in it. It may be that the most appropriate vantage point from which to experience your work is from a distance, say fifty feet, because of your need for psychic distance between your autobiographical work and the attentions of your audience. Or the most effective vantage point may be a tight circle, a few feet from the work, this distance and arrangement being best to create the necessary degree of intimacy and solidarity you desire from your audience. Whatever the viewing circumstances desired, it is important to exercise your artistic discretion here to determine the forum within which your work is best experienced. This done, you may also determine how your companions are to verbally react to your work, with the primary objective of the exchange being the expansion of depth and complexity of meaning the work has for you. Under some circumstances it might benefit you most to simply listen to your peers' reactions upon witnessing your work, and for you to offer no rejoinders, no explanations, neither agreement nor disagreement. You have given them your work; it is a language of forms. In return they have given you a verbal impression of what they think and feel as a consequence of having witnessed your work. This view of the reflection of someone else's mind is an extraordinary opportunity to see ourselves, this time from the other side of our skin and through the imagining and observing of another. Or you may wish to ask questions that you are wrestling with about your work, focusing the concerns of your companion upon those of your own. Further still, you may wish to invite an exchange of views, soliciting differing personal interpretations of elements common to the works of all those present. Or still further, you may elect to have the work witnessed in mutual silence or accompanied by a monologue from you. Remember, it is your prerogative to determine the circumstances under which your work will be seen and engaged in by others; these circumstances ought to be designed so as to bring you maximum clarity and discovery of meaning in your own work.

Whatever format you choose, certain elements will require particular attention in the interaction between you and your companions. Many people at some point focus on the associated meanings embedded in the objects themselves. For instance, you may speak of this black shiny rock standing for the darkness of your stubborness, and this string representing your resiliency. In addition to looking at the meaning residing in each object, it is also instructive to notice the meanings that derive from the placement of those objects—the meaning residing in the composition, the grammar of the work. Eight objects arranged to form a three-foot square represent quite a different person than if those same eight objects were randomly strewn across a twenty-foot-long swath of material. Similarly, a composition set indoors in a corner of a darkened room suggests quite a different meaning than it would if that same composition were placed in the center of the room, or the center of a doorway, or the center of a meadow. *Where* a thing is is as meaningful as *what* the thing is. Recognizing the meanings that reside in the contextual level of the work is often surprisingly revealing for the artist, because we are not as accustomed to "reading" intervals as we are objects.

Processing

The following questions may help you to tease meaning from intangibles of space and proximity.

- If you would move one item closer (farther) away from the others, how would that be less (more) you?
- If one item were eliminated from (added to) the composition, how would that be less (more) the person you see yourself as?
- How would the meaning of the piece be altered if you rotated a particular object in the composition?
- What would you do to change this work to be more (less) the person you would like to be?

Designed—as all these exercises are—to provide the highest degree of accessibility, this encounter requires absolutely no trained technique, no prior knowledge of art in any fashion. As such, it serves well as an initial experience. Each response is distinctive, each is made in privacy and shared in public on the artist's own terms. It is an exercise that invites candor, a sharing of things of importance, and it invites ways of speaking and listening that are as rare as they are rewarding. This is a particularly useful introductory encounter because the many expressive choices to be made will most likely be new to the participants and thus allow for a revealing freshness in the work. Many important and touching aspects of the self are portrayed in this encounter, which as a consequence of the group discussion will begin to build a strong peer support system for each member. Several important events have likely occurred, nurturing our creative expressiveness and shaping the working environment so as to enhance the exercise of our creative potential.

1. Most importantly, you have turned inward for your responses, consulting your sense of self for the appropriate reactions.
2. You have employed both your deliberate intelligence and your intuitive, somatic intelligence.
3. You have created works that hold important meanings for you, and have brought these meanings to the attention of others.
4. Others have "seen" important dimensions of you and spoken directly to you of their awareness of these qualities.
5. You have used things, space, and circumstances and shaped them to your own desires and thereby reshaped the world, albeit in a modest way, as an outcome of your desires.
6. You have attended to others as they have undergone similar trials and resolutions, and now you share something of particular value with others. A bond of trust and support is being woven between you and the world. This is all to the good.

SEEKING YOUR NATURAL MARK

It is difficult to speak about yourself using a borrowed language. This is so because language is not a passive instrument through which information neutrally flows. Language not only carries meaning; language *is* meaning. Each word has its own history, its own key users and events. Language triggers off climates of meanings because words and their usage are born in particular settings. Words do not simply expose mind; words are the stuff from which minds are constructed. Language captures selected portions of what is "out there," setting us on a particular course that predisposes us to meet only certain things "out there" and "in here" while veiling all the rest. Not simply words, but grammar, syntax, intonation, pronunciation are means of declaring what is real and what is good. The poets and writers who bring us real news are those who wrest language from the background noise of our living and bring it forward into consciousness, shaping it to their own ends.

Black American writers realized this in the flowering of their literature in the sixties. They understood that they could not think about themselves as they knew themselves to be by employing the thinking (speaking/writing) of the white majority. They could not do so because the thinking of whites concerning blacks was in the main pejorative and steeped in a history of humiliation and forced submission. The very word *black* has sinister, mysterious, anxious overtones in the white lexicon. The words *boy, girl, sister, brother,* mostly neutral terms for whites, were respectively searing and humiliating or comforting and empowering for blacks.

Appropriating the language of the dominating class to speak of things that are precious to one's own self and kind—that is, the very things held in contempt by the dominant class—is to defeat at the outset the aim of speaking fully and respectfully of one's own self and kind. Appreciating the interactive quality of language, especially in the hands of an artist, Rollo May says,

> W. H. Auden once remarked to me in private conversation: "The poet marries the language, and out of this marriage the poem is born." How *active* this makes the language in the creation of a poem! It is not that language is merely a tool of communication, or that we only use language to express our ideas; it is just as true that language uses *us.*[26]

In the knowledge of this basic truth, black literature, Chicano literature, American Indian literature, Jewish literature, and women's literature have risen and flowered.

Language is power. Language is mind. Language is access to history, to a chosen future. Language provides a space in which we can be ourselves and be with the people of our choosing. We must have a language at our disposal that fits our own aspirations, a language that declares the legitimacy of our presence in the world, our style of living. For those born to the majority, their language speaks kindly of their past, affirmatively about their present, and hopefully about their future. Fortunate people, these, in their own ways. But not all occupy the center and come from the mainstream. And in some real way we *all* are on the periphery. No one has exactly walked our way before. If we are to make a full accounting of how this life appears to us, borrowed words will not do; we must forge our own terms for our special news. It becomes ever more clear that if we are to bring the news to the center from the edges, we must speak the news in our own voice.

Encounter

In the following exercise we are not so much interested in the exploration of an *issue* as we are in discovering our natural use of *language,* our natural mark. We want to explore how our personal predispositions, residing as they do at a subliminal level, naturally and unself-consciously manifest themselves in the gestures of our hand.

We seek gestures that emerge from a quiet and deep place within. Since the inside is so overlayered by a thick and resistant crust of acquired stylistic flourishes, we have to find a way to set aside this barrier and draw upon the deeper levels of our sense of self. Frankly, we have to outwit our ever-vigilant rational mind with all its ready-made signs and behaviors. We will attempt to do this by initially heading down a path that seems innocuous enough so as not to alarm our conscious mind. Our effort will be to travel this road long enough to uncover all-but-forgotten domains, and to take note of what we encounter along the way. Our rational mind will soon awaken to what is going on and will try to bring us back to familiar, if stale, territory. But if we are determined to push on with our own becoming, we are more than likely to gain some foothold on this original landscape and derive reward from this first, Promethean step.

Phase 1. Wander about seeking natural things—plants, stones, bones— whose pattern of *growth* is apparent, and which have some eye-catching, special appeal for you. Allow your eyes to pass over the landscape, registering what they take in rather than seeking out predetermined forms. You will find what you need, often with some surprise at what appeals or doesn't appeal to you. Collect about half a dozen such natural things whose *rhythm* and *pattern* have this appeal for you. For example, suppose an oak leaf catches our fancy. The energy is extruded from the branch through the stem of the leaf and, like a river plain, spreads out in a particular, fanlike pattern, ending its journey in sharp points and rounded bays. The channels are clear, crisp, short, angular. The bays and points come at regular intervals. The central, internal force seems to thrust the object forward into its pattern or form. In the objects that appeal to you, watch for where the energy seems to enter the form, how it courses through that form and eventuates into the outer edges.

Having found six or so objects that move you, bring them together and arrange them on a flat surface so as to best display each one's energy, pattern, rhythm. Having done this, notice what that rhythm looks like and how your body responds to that rhythm.

Phase 2. Look more closely at one piece that seems to particularly embody a rhythm that feels right to you. Spend a few minutes allowing your eye to follow the rhythm of the piece. Allow your eyes to course along the piece as the course of energy pulses through it. Now close your eyes and continue to "see" the movement in your mind's eye. Open your eyes again to confirm and deepen that movement. Again closing your eyes, follow the movement in your visual memory. Bring what was seen on the outside within, to be experienced somatically, inside. Now let one of your hands trace that same movement in the air, coordinating the movement of your mind's eye with the movements of your hand. Repeat this until there is an easy synchronization between your mind's eye and your hand.

Phase 3. Still with your eyes closed, continue your hand movements, this time touching the surface of the paper. Feel your hand coursing over the paper, be sensitive to the varying pressures, changes in direction, and changes in velocity as your hand takes account of the rhythms of your eyes and your eyes take account of the rhythms of the original object.

Phase 4. Now, still with your eyes closed, take up a piece of chalk or pastel and, allowing the chalk to be an extension of your hand, touch it down on the paper, continuing the original movement. Once again, be aware of what you feel in your fingertips, in your shoulders, and now what you hear as the chalk glides and scrapes across the surface of the paper. When you have done this for a while and feel the full rhythm of the gesture as natural and comfortable, effortless, open your eyes *without* altering the movement of your hands. Simply and passively observe your hand dancing across the paper, leaving a trail of marks. Watch your hand move as if it were not your own, as you would watch a dancer on a stage. Watch the emerging lines being left behind by your hand as it caresses the page with the edge of the chalk.

Phase 5. Keeping the movement going, substitute a new piece of paper for the old, this time allowing your hand to improvise, extend, play with the

original movement and subsequent line. Try not to interfere too much here with your deliberate mind; like a loving, indulgent parent, just allow your hand to "go outside and play."

Phase 6. By this time your other hand has probably become quite jealous of just watching its mirror twin having such a good time, so why not bring this other hand into the action? One way to do this is to have the other hand join the first hand, so that they move across the paper together holding the one piece of chalk. After getting the hang of things, give your first hand a breather, and allow the second hand to solo. Having grown up on the other side of town, this hand probably has a somewhat different view of things. Allow this hand to experiment with and discover its own rhythms and flourishes, rates and pressures.

Phase 7. Perhaps now, on yet another paper, have both hands work simultaneously, again allowing each to be as close or as distant to each other in gesture as they desire. Keep playing, exploring, improvising. When you feel you have pushed this as far as you desire, stop and assemble all the images and survey your journey.

Processing

Much of this encounter was experienced with your eyes closed and/or in an unpredetermined frame of mind. You may now ask yourself the following questions to help you focus in on the experience's conceptual gains.

- Just what is distinctive about the rhythms you found so appealing in the object you selected?
- What happened as you internalized those "found" rhythms and then externalized them?
- How are the marks you made like the marks that you make on life, on the course you steer through life?
- What's new here, what is old?
- How are the marks of your left hand different from your right? How are they similar?
- In what way did you extend your movements and marks when you were invited to do so?
- Are there some marks that resemble other movements, gestures, conceptual styles of yourself?
- Turn the images in various directions (upside down, etc.). Does any orientation feel "truer" than any other? How?—and, perhaps, why?

Extensions. Having explored these natural marks based upon one object, you may now want to explore this entire process using another natural object, one exhibiting different rhythms and patterns.

This series primarily used line to portray (record) your natural rhythm and mark. You may also explore the same general idea by introducing color, texture, composition, or shape. Chalk or pastel were used here for convenience' sake, but you could use a variety of paints, or even a slab of clay. Each medium will promote a different range of marks (language) to be represented and will therefore reveal a further dimension of your self.

A further extension of this general point of view is to make a full-length self-portrait in the form of a landscape. Taking stock of your natural rhythms, textures, tones, values, colors, and shapes, create a landscape metaphor for the person you take yourself to be. And perhaps as a further extension, this time going back to the natural setting from which you originally selected your natural objects, place your painted landscape in a natural setting that also speaks of you. Are you nighttime, sunset, sunrise? Are you winter, spring, fall meadow giving way to winter woodlands? Are you August, May? Seeing your handiwork within a portion of the world that echoes and reinforces your work creates a kind of bond between you and the world, reveals an underlying kinship. The sense of being a natural member of the world, the sense of belonging, engenders an empowering sense of self. By discovering our natural marks we discover a means to speak powerfully and fully about things that matter to us. Natural, belonging, in tune with the universe, empowered: this is what we want.

GOING TO THE INFINITE WELL

We usually traverse the same territory each day, making our rounds in typical fashion. That's what makes us *us*. And for the most part, that is all to the good. It's also comforting and efficient. There are times, however, when familiar paths and ways keep us stuck in patterns no longer rewarding. This exercise encourages us to traverse new territory in new ways while minimizing the usual anxiety about doing so. It also cultivates a light hand and an uncomplicated, nimble mind. Its rapid pace cuts through our usual convoluted thinking, and the large number of mini-tasks called for soon overwhelms our ordinary repertoire of responses, calling forth unexpected reservoirs of original and personal responses.

Encounter

The exercise has three phases; each phase has its own characteristics, but all three are linked necessarily with one another.

Phase 1. Embark on a hunt, with no specific quarry in mind except that it should be an object, either human-made or naturally occurring, whose features in some fashion "speak to you." Don't concern yourself just now about *why* the object speaks to you (or about what); it is sufficient to simply take up what appeals to you. Wander about for a while to this end, wherever you like. At some point something will catch your fancy, and when it does, nab it.

When this is done, set up next to you in handy fashion about a hundred sheets of paper—not large, eight-by-ten-inch sheets will do—and plenty of simple drawing media: chalks, crayons, charcoal. Now spend a little while looking carefully at the object you have selected. Look at it, touch it, know it so well that it now belongs to your mind's eye. Putting the object out of sight, and allowing the experience of looking at this object to swirl around in your head, you will in another moment create images expressive of your reaction to "meeting" the object to which you were drawn. But wait, another word on this.

A key artifice of this exercise is the brevity and frequency of your responses. The less time you allow yourself to reflect on how to approach the task, the less confined you are likely to be by old standard responses. The more rapidly you do this exercise, the more quickly you will exhaust your usual repertoire of image making and the sooner you are likely to wander into new territory. Therefore, each new image will be given only sixty seconds to come forward before you then go on to the next work without pausing. Having spent sixty seconds creating the first work, an image based on your reaction to seeing the original object, go right on to the next drawing. This subsequent drawing will be expressive of your reaction to your *previous drawing*, and should also be drawn in sixty seconds. Keep repeating this pattern of sixty-second images, each new drawing based on the experience of having made the previous drawing, *fifty-eight more times.* To keep the flow going uninterruptedly and evenly, it is good to have a timekeeper or some other kind of automatic device that indicates the time, perhaps by ringing a small bell every sixty seconds.

When the hour is up, stop. One hour of this will be exhausting! You may have experienced a number of reactions as you moved through the exercise, from increasing exhilaration to decreasing energy and increasing frustration. Be aware of your bodily reactions at each stage of the series, note at what phase of the exercise you ran out of ideas, got stuck, became frustrated, got your second wind, made an exhilarating breakthrough, or were swept along by fresh inspirations.

Phase 2. It is important to take a ten-minute break now before going on with the next phase of the exercise, in order to recenter and recoup your strength. Breathe long and deep, allow your mind to survey the experiences of the last hour. And then let it all go. Having cleared your mind and refocused your energies, assemble all of your work in a chronological order so that the entire collection can be seen in one sweep and the evolution of the series can be noticed. If you are working with others, it will be most revealing to view your work in the context of your companions' work.

As you peruse the collection of your work, note the following characteristics of the series as a whole:

- The *direction* of the evolution of the pieces: have you moved toward more abstraction/realism, toward more gesture/detail, toward more/less color, texture, pattern?
- The *distance* between images: how much of a difference is there between one image and the next? Was the pattern of change drastic, or moderate? What *kinds* of changes did you make in mood, attitude, approach, conception?
- The *fatigue* factor: did you run out of ordinary responses after a while and probe any new territory?
- How did you handle your fatigue, your breathless pace, your frustration, your out-of-controlness? Did you meet your fatigue in anger, in a welcome yielding, in defeat, perhaps in soft joy?
- Your reaction(s) to the *time* constraints: Did you make it into an enemy, an ally, or an opportunity?
- Did you uncover some very old ways of working?
- Did you discover any new ways of working?

If you were working with others, you may ask yourself about the unique characteristics of your work, your evolution, the gestalt of your entire series in relation to the others. In what ways was your series unique? What characteristics do you share with someone else? with all others?

*Phase 3.*Having completed this first series of explorations, select *one* image from the previous sixty that somehow seems pregnant with possibilities yet to be explored. With this as your model, make a reactive image that develops the model image further, pushes it somehow further along. Take five minutes for this effort. After you have made this work, notice the conventions you employed in creating it. A convention is a particular way of doing something: for example, the particular color spectrum you employed, the slant, number, and presence of strokes, the degree of abstraction, the predominant line quality or texture or shape. These are all conventions, particular ways of working. Having recognized the conventions you employed in creating the work, then select *one* such rule, and somehow break it in the creation of a new work. For example, you may have used a tight range of colors in your first piece to create a sense of orderliness. To break that convention you may decide to employ an aggressively wide palette of colors. Do this convention-breaking exercise at least five times, creating a work, noticing a convention, breaking that convention in the making of the new work, and taking about five minutes to do each one.

After the series has run its course, once again assemble the works so that the whole can be subsumed in one look and the chronology of their evolution can be seen as well.

You might reflect on this series with the help of the following questions.

- Did you operate differently in this series than in the previous one? If so, how and why? How is a five-minute span more or less conducive for you in boundary breaking, in concern for craftsmanship, in the exercise of your imagination, in your rhythm of working?
- What categories of conventions did you select to break and change? Which did you keep intact (e.g., color, line, texture, velocity, etc.)?
- How great a change did you permit yourself between works?
- What new conventions did you begin to employ?
- What powers seem now to have resided in each convention that became more apparent to you as you gave it up?
- What new powers did you acquire as a result of creating and employing new conventions?

Once again, if you are working in the company of others, reflect on the special way you go about doing things silhouetted against the ways of others. To become familiar with your natural ways is to hear your natural voice, speak your native tongue. This is intrinsically empowering and helps to extend your creative range beyond convention and habit.

Phase 4. Finally, select one work from this last series that seems to you to have *broken new ground.* This work should not be the most accomplished or most resolved, but rather the work that seems to hold the most promise—not least because it does seem so unresolved and challenging. Now, in this next undertaking, take up those challenges and chase them as far as you can, entering as fully as you can the new territory that the earlier work only pointed toward. See what happens when you devote more time to this enterprise. Take half an hour to an hour for this final phase of the series.

Upon completion of the work, again view it slowly and deliberately. As you do, you might consider the following questions.

- Given thirty to sixty times the amount of time first allotted in this series to engage in a creative enterprise, how have you employed your talents? Have you given yourself over to crafting a well-made thing? Have you become more constrained with such ample time to think between strokes?
- Has the increase of time-space provided more opportunity for depth of feeling, intricacy of image, subtlety of effect?
- Have you used this increase of time to also increase your scale, your palette, your dexterity, your thoughts? Or have you actually been restricted by this new, lush environment? Have you become too heady with possibilities and, like Hamlet, failed to act with dispatch even though your cause has been worthy?

Observations. Time and repetition have been used as both invitations and constraints in this series of exercises in the service of allowing old ways to be let go and new ways to be tried out. The reward for engaging in these exercises is rather paradoxical. The old and ordinary ways of working, once exposed and eventually run through, usually turn out to be acquired ways, learned from societal conventions. They are ours, but they are borrowed. The new ways of working, emergent from the collapse of the old and ordinary, turn out to be not really so much new as primal or indigenous. These newly emerged indigenous ways of image making often seem to have expressive poignancy and to flow more naturally than the cultivated, acquired conventions we have been used to employing and which we took to be ourselves. It takes a while to become acquainted with this newly uncovered language. Once we do so, however, the ease and depth of expression will be remarkably evident.

VISUAL DIALOGUES

Most of the time we are engaged with others through the exchange of spoken words. What we say and what we hear create the major portion of our social reality. Because talk is the thing we do most with others, it is only natural that much of this talk has become ritualized. We address others and attend to others in whole, prepared clumps of verbiage. We expect certain things to be said by certain people on certain occasions. Once begun, a whole string of statements and responding statements will run its course, carrying little original news or interest. Society expects this of us, and we expect it of others. We are known by others, even by ourselves, by the typicality of our conversation. It is both a comfort and a trap, for our language does as much to conceal the person who we really feel ourselves to be as it does to reveal. It is difficult to be the emergent person we know we are becoming when the words we have to express this are old and the expected words others wish to hear us say will no longer do. We need a new way of speaking if we are to speak of new things.

The following exercise employs another language with which to engage in dialogue. Unlike our verbal language, this language has no prior existence, has never been spoken before, nor has it been heard. It requires therefore the utmost attentiveness of both the speaker and the listener. It requires creativity, caring, patience, and subtlety. It also cultivates these same traits in turn.

Instead of speaking standard words within the structure of a conventional grammar, you will be creating marks having unique symbolic meaning and composing these marks in units and patterns according to conventions of your own device. Your partner will be doing the same. The miracle is that you will understand each other—but, miraculously, you will.

Encounter

As its title suggests, this exercise is a dialogue between two parties; therefore you need to have a partner. Every partnership engaging in this exercise will derive its own particular language and generate its own particular conversation based upon the relationship of the two parties. One would naturally expect very different dynamics and outcomes from a parent working with his or her offspring than those from partners who are a married couple, old friends, or new acquaintances—and indeed the results are different. *Who* you work with will therefore be a significant factor in this exercise. All partnerships are revealing and rewarding in their own ways. So try this often, with a variety of partners.

A rather large single sheet of paper, shared between the partners, and an assortment of easy-to-use materials, dry or wet, are the cheap and easy media required.

Phase 1. The dynamics used to set this exercise in motion are quite simple but essential for maximizing its potential profits.

1. Both partners work on the single sheet of paper between them. As in any conversation, one partner begins with some kind of opening "line," a line that is both expressive of how it is going just now and a line that in some fashion invites a response. Putting the paintbrush or other medium down signals that the point to be expressed has been made and that it is now the turn of the other partner to offer a rejoinder.
2. Only one partner works at a time, while the other closely follows the action.
3. No talking throughout the exercise. Verbal talk only diminishes the expressiveness of the visual dialogue.
4. A preset, relatively short period of time works best; different time spans will promote varying degrees of intimacy, complexity, and subtlety of exchange. Dialogues lasting a total of less than five minutes often are shallow or hurried; ones that go on for longer than fifteen minutes usually collapse upon themselves in overelaborateness or verbosity. If the conversation has run its course sooner than the allotted time, stop as soon as it feels complete to both partners.
5. The simpler the media, the better; complex materials such as oil paints divert the focus from expression to performance.

Now decide who will initiate the conversation, and then begin.

Phase 2. Immediately after completing the visual dialogue, each partner will most likely feel a compelling need to speak to the other about his or her experience. So do it. Much has been exchanged in this dialogue, some things probably for the first time; therefore it is important that some private time and space be provided to share whatever is deemed important. You have been addressed in ways that may have affirmed or inadvertently overlooked a very delicate and essential personal quality. You have most likely done the same to your partner. You have been "heard"—and perhaps not listened to—in very sensitive areas, and so was your partner. You have each played, teased, invited, rebuffed each other in a new language that has perhaps penetrated new regions. You can now extend and synthesize those visual and tactile experiences by literally voicing what transpired for you.

Here are some questions to help you to extract full potential from this exercise.

- What role did you play in this exchange? Were you, in the main, the initiator of images (color, line, formats), or were you an elaborator, or a follower, or a challenger?
- How much territory did your portion of the exchange occupy? How close to you was your domain, how close to your partner, how clumped together or widespread?
- How often and in what ways did you allow your lines to touch the lines of your partner? How close did you allow your lines to come to those of your partner? Did you make your lines parallel, did you cross lines, did you ignore lines, did you extend or elaborate or simplify your partner's lines?
- What did you do to make yourself understood?
- How did you attempt to understand your partner?
- Was this work for you, or play, a time to share intimacies, a display of power or dominance, a display of cleverness, skill?
- What did you have to deny yourself as a consequence of sharing space with another, what did you have to negotiate, assert, claim, grab?
- How did it feel to be "seen" by your partner? Not to be seen?
- Did you adapt any of your ways as a consequence of seeing your partner's work? Did your partner do so?
- What in fact did you "talk" about?

Phase 3. The "conversation" you just had was conducted under certain imposed constraints—no talking while drawing, one partner working at a time, and so on. Your conversation therefore in some way reflected those impositions. Now, working with the same partner, decide what conditions you both feel would be more propitious for the exercise. Work on a smaller or larger surface, change media, work simultaneously, whatever. Discuss, decide, and go to it.

Phase 4. Once again, allow the visual dialogue to run its course. After its completion, together share your experiences.

To process this dialogue, you might want to ask yourself and discuss with your partner the following questions:

- How did this exchange differ from the first?
- Which factors influenced the outcome this time?
- How was this different for you? What did you do this time that was different from the first time?
- How did your mind-set this time result in different rewards than the first time?
- How do you feel about your partner and your partnership this time?

Extensions. Certain variations on this same theme can further extend your expressiveness and your ability to assert your own mind and presence without compromising and also without disallowing your partner to do likewise. Having worked with your partner and become acquainted with his or her style of working under certain limited circumstances, you might now try some of the following variations:

- resolve to be a *mentor* to your partner, helping him or her to bring forth a desired characteristic.
- resolve to be more the person you really are.
- resolve to be a more attentive, responsive partner.
- resolve to be more playful, adventurous.
- assume a different persona, one you would like to try on, see how it fits.

These visual dialogues will most likely generate an expanded range of visual vocabulary for you, a working vocabulary whose effectiveness and expressive powers may now be more apparent to you. By adding these natural marks to your vocabulary, you have opened a new range of means by which you may speak to others about how the world appears to you.

Speaking in a new language allows you to account for aspects of the universe that are probably left out by your conventional way of speaking. More to the point, speaking in a new language allows you to actually *perceive* a wider and more subtle range of the universe both "out there" and "in here." The extended self this leads to in turn can't help but lead to a more expansive life and to creative endeavors that are equally expansive. Just what we want. Note, however, that these visual dialogues reveal only the territory that lies between any two souls. Each soul being unique, the territory created between them is also unique. So practice this encounter often; it will always reveal an expanded world and self.

FORBIDDEN COLORS

Some time ago I came upon a chapter title that struck me to the quick in a work by Yukio Mishima. I had been working for a while on a series of drawings that were becoming ever more tedious just as I was becoming ever more frustrated. I could not wrench myself out of using old ways to address new concerns. Consequently, the efforts looked and felt forced: certainly they seemed self-conscious. Then I came upon this phrase in Mishima's book: "Forbidden Colors."

As such things happen, what was elusive and murky one moment became utterly clear and fully formed the next. It was now apparent to me that my stuckedness wasn't my failure to use well what I had; it was a failure of my imagination to allow me access to the full range of possibilities (of color, this time) within which whole new domains of thinking and gesture resided. The problem was, I had forbidden myself to employ a range of colors (it could have been lines or shapes or what have you) that could speak of things I wished to say but could not convey without those colors.

Forbidden colors indeed! I was not interested just then in knowing why I had cut myself off from this other world; that I had forbidden myself certain sights and uncertain pleasures was impetus enough for me to change all that. And I did. I closed the book, drove to the art store, went right to those Pandora's trays of pastels, started at the top drawer and pulled it open. There they were, dozens and dozens of tints and shades of one color. The first tray happened to have all yellows. Sour yellows, cool yellows, citrus yellows, bitter yellows. All there, innocent, feigning sleep. I went right across the silent columns in the tray. If a color repelled me, I took it. If I had never used that hue or tint or shade before, I nabbed it. A handful of forbidden yellows!

Then on to the next tray. Ah, greens. Nasty python greens, celadon sublime greens, bean greens, greens wanting to be blue, dirt greens, eye greens. Again I snatched these forbidden beauties and shoved them in my bag. Now blues, then browns, and reds, even a tray of grays. I ravished them all. It cost me a fortune in their purchase. It had cost me a fortune in their denial.

Then back to my studio, the great sack of forbidden colors now jammed altogether under my arm. The hubbub they were making in there! An expansive sheet of open-faced paper tacked to the wall, the bag of colors opened, I plunged my hand in.

Who would be first? First one, then others eluded my grasp, but my fingers finally closed on a somewhat slower one, I had it by the scruff of its miserable neck. I withdrew my hand, and there it was, a cylinder crammed

132

with the palest blue. So weak, fragile, and self-effacing, hardly blue at all. All the usual brashness of blue drained away. If it had a place in the sky, it was at the edges of the day, maybe a late August morning after a steamy, heavy night. A tired sigh of blue. No wonder I had never bothered with it before, the puny little thing.

But now, on closer inspection, there was something quite appealing in its shyness. You could get close to this blue without being overwhelmed, slammed in the face by its blueness. There was a feeling of failed aristocracy here. Appealing to me, a lad originally from Brooklyn. Well, now to touch it to the paper, see what will out. And I did.

Encounter

The exploration of forbidden territory brings rewards quite distinct from the exploration of remote domains. Canvassing what is distant acquaints us with all that is outside our ken. We come back full of ideas and new ways, and the challenge is not simply to accumulate these things but to apply them to the life that we have.

Forbidden territory is different from remote territory. Whereas the remote contains unknown material that beckons to the eager traveler, forbidden territory contains material known but rejected. The confrontation with our own antipathy and the chance to reclaim what we may have too hastily rejected are the rewards of this exercise.

It is worth looking at the forbidden domain a bit further. Rejection derives from prior experience that we now bring to bear on current events. Some of the reasoning behind our taboos is sound, so that we still do well to avoid the material. Some of it, however, has outlived its usefulness and now only serves to keep us from what might be ours. In fact, if we really rejected the material outright it would cease to have fascination for us. Thus we want to explore the material that still has a compelling quality, even if the direction of the fascination is away rather than toward us. We want to reopen the case, find out if there are qualities we are pushing away that we might do better to embrace. After all, it is we who have forbidden ourselves to engage these areas. We have closed the door, built the wall. Nowadays very few items on our forbidden list come to us directly from society. Most of what we don't traffic in is self-imposed, and we can always close the door on this domain again. However, we will never know how viable our boundaries are if we do not, from time to time, test them. The following exercise provides such an opportunity, a time to reexamine paths not taken and see where the trail may now lead.

A Brief Note on Color. This experience of exploring forbidden territory focuses on using color as the key element. Of course we could also reexamine other elements such as line quality, theme, value, tone, scale, stroke, image, and so on. I highly recommend that you do so, for all elements are bounded by our sense of self and propriety and all therefore may be expanded.

I have chosen to focus here on color, by way of example, for several reasons. Color contains inherent personality. Ultramarine blue stands differently in the world than does Naples yellow, no matter who picks up the tube. Working with color immediately sets up a dialogue between us and that color. Line, form, shape wait upon us for their creation, color precedes us. If in the following exercise we continue to overwhelm this "other," refuse it in the right to display its personality, our world will remain exactly as large and as deep as before, and we will simply have erased a few more minutes of our life. If, however, we allow color to have its say without censorship, we may find that it speaks about things that are important for us to attend to. The color may also speak a rhythm and melody that turn out to strike us quite deeply. These heretofore forbidden colors may also allow us to address themes we previously forbade ourselves and approach them from vantage points otherwise inaccessible.

Phase 1. The procedure for this exercise is straightfoward enough. Select or mix up a batch of colors you ordinarily *wouldn't* use. The further these colors are from those you find tasteful and attractive, the better. In fact, try hard to find or make a color that is positively repulsive. We want the energy contained in repulsion. Start with just one such color and let it run its course. It is imperative here not to be judgmental. As I have urged elsewhere, allow your eye to passively acknowledge what is displayed as the color leaves its nasty trail on the paper. Play with that color, tease it, challenge it, squash it, dare it, let it attack you, push it this way and that, a little warmer, a little cooler, more red, less blue, chase it all over the place, let it say *its* piece. Try this with several colors, one at a time. Don't attempt to derive conclusions from what you are doing at this point, simply allow things to happen, witness them without imposing your usual mindfulness.

Phase 2. When you have explored the voices and personalities of the "forbidden" colors to your satisfaction, experiment with another series of markings, this time using two or three colors together. Expanding your palette in terms of hue, tint, and value will expose whole new vocabularies of the other elements as well, such as line, form, mass, and so on. Keeping the expanded palette to two or three colors at a time will allow you to discern the individual personality of each contributing color with a minimum of confusion.

Processing

When these experiments have run their course, this would be a good time to assemble the whole of your efforts and spend a while familiarizing yourself with each one and with the collection as a whole. It may help to ask yourself the following questions:
- Which "forbidden" colors actually provided access to propitious new territory?
- Which ones seem as repulsive now as they did before?
- Which seemed to engage your fascination, which deepened your thoughts?
- Which colors seem now to be more natural to you than you had anticipated?
- Which colors, in combination, mixed or side by side, excite you with their power of expression?
- Which allow you to say new things?
- Which allow you to say old things but in new and deeper ways?
- Other surprises, other confirmations?

After reflecting upon your own work, it may also be useful to work with one or two other people, reflecting back to one another what you saw in your own work and one another's work. When you are working on uncovering/discovering things that lie very close to you, you are often the last person to know what it is you have just found.

The title of this encounter is "Forbidden Colors," but it is not so much about colors as it is about breaking out of any self-imposed and unnecessarily constricting pattern of thinking. That's what we want to address: the releasing of our potential creative spirit from the confines of ordinary thinking. When we do exceed our self-imposed limitations, the increase of vitality, well-being, and creative appetite is our substantial reward.

As a final encounter with this newly explored palette of colors, you would do well to employ them in a new work. Perhaps this time introduce them to old standby friends—colors you habitually use. See if you can find a way to love these new members of your expanded family. See if they don't allow you to account for a wider range of feelings and ideas than you could have expressed before. See what happens when this new vocabulary meets this emergent you. You might have some very important business together.

YIN/YANG

Creativity requires the availability of a great deal of uncommitted energy simply to overcome the inertia of coping with the world exactly as it is. It requires even more energy to ultimately imagine a new world and to fabricate it. Therefore, the more we are able to employ our available energy in the services of creative enterprises, the more likely we are to propel our imagination forward and find the way to fabricate our dreams. The following encounter aims to invigorate our available creative capacities by bringing together what modern Western civilization has sundered, our pool of masculine and feminine energies.

Chinese philosophy posits that there are two basic universal and complementary forces in nature; working as two halves of a whole, they give the world its particular spin. All things have some degree of both these energies, which create their particular life force, dynamic tension, and symmetry. Unlike our prevailing Western ideas of reality, which tend to focus on the dominant characteristic of any one element while neglecting the recessive characteristics, the Eastern view tends to focus on the dynamic relation of the two basic forces in every thing and every event. *Yin* and *Yang* are the terms given to these universal forces. Conventionally yin is the female principle or quality: it predominates in the earth and in water; its nature is manifest in its flexibility, wholeness, coolness, endurance, and so on. Yang is found in heat and geometry; it is oaken, rigid, assertive, outward reaching; it is the male principle.

In the West we too recognize these two basic forces as the characteristic qualities of the two genders. In the West, however, we tend to see the two forces as opposing one another, arising from two distinct origins and coursing through the world as two quite complete and self-sufficient entities. Yin/yang perspectives, by contrast, recognize the necessity of each for the other. The yin is the completion of the yang, and vice versa. Yin and yang complement each other, require each other, yearn for each other, bring each other to fruition. Carl Jung, for example, speaks of the yin/yang complementarity in human affairs in terms of the anima and animus. We seek in our life partners that shadow self that will complete our being. It is the dynamic relationship between our masculine and feminine characteristics that we seek to foster in this encounter.

Our interest as artists in this way of viewing the forces that animate the universe arises because these two forces are the same forces that animate us. More to our point, they are the basic creative forces in the universe and, as such, once recognized as dynamic components of ourselves, may be employed singly or together for our own desired creative endeavors.

Encounter

Our aims in the following encounter are to gain a clearer appreciation of the degree of yin and yang we currently have, to notice how these two forces manifest themselves in our work and in our everyday life, and—if there is a deficit in one—to seek ways to rectify that imbalance. If we are oblivious to the naturally occurring patterns of energy that animate us or even attempt to work against them, we dissipate our available portion of energy by fighting against our natural predisposition. Not realizing that we do have a natural pattern shaped by the particular proportions of yin and yang, we exhaust ourselves thinking that our shallow and pallid artistic efforts are a failure of our creative artistic abilities. We berate ourselves for having so little imagination, so little talent. It may be nothing of the kind. Our neutralized creative energies may be the way they are only because we have failed to work in harmony with our natural pattern of energy flow, our yin/yang dynamic balance. The thing is first to recognize the powers that animate us and then to find ways to work with those natural and inward-dwelling powers to create a portion (tiny as it may be) of the universe to our liking. Since these two forces are always in dynamic tension, fusing in one observable behavior, if we are to notice each, we need to tease one away from the other. We can do this by exaggerating one, allowing our body to register its reaction to the presence of now one, now the other.

Phase 1. Although this exercise may be done on one's own, it is best realized by working with a partner or group. Working in partnership allows you to manifest, for instance, the yin principle while your partner resists or supports you by exhibiting yang powers. Reversing roles, mirroring, exaggerating each principle by working with another allows the characteristics of these powers to be made more conspicuous and, ultimately, more available. The description of the yin/yang encounter will be given for two people working as partners. If you are working alone or in a large group, you may easily modify the instructions accordingly.

Yin's strength resides in its being flexible, fluid, oceanic, flowing, cool, inward. Yang's power resides in its durability, inflexibility, heat, outwardness, single-mindedness.

Walk across the room in a manner expressive of your yang energy, straight, unswerving, erect, determined, angular. Notice how it feels to walk in this fashion, watch yourself as you come up against others, notice your breathing and how you hold your frame. Notice the places of tension: in your hands, jaw, abdomen, neck, back. Notice, too, the effect others have upon you as they enter your pathway, notice what happens to them and to you as you are compelled to avoid one another.

As you stride about the room in yang fashion, try on some other yang characteristics; experience yourself as hot, dry, oaken, durable, deliberate. Notice where your center seems to be located, how high up in your body, in what limbs, organs. Watch your breathing all throughout this exercise, make it audible, perhaps put a sound to it corresponding to your breathing.

As you continue to yang-walk, exaggerate the motion of your arms. Don't change the style of movement, just extend it somewhat past the normal range so that you bring it to conscious awareness. After five minutes of yang movements, stop and rest a bit. Be aware of your body sensations, your muscular vitality, your temperature. Be aware of the emotional state you are now experiencing and the thoughts and images that are coursing through your mind. Center yourself now and just relax, let the yang energy flow out until it has ebbed and you are feeling somewhat neutral. A series of deep, controlled breaths with eyes closed and in a motionless position will help to bring you to a neutral condition. Proceed with the next phase when you feel yourself to be at rest.

Now repeat the general series of walking, breathing, sense-awareness exercises carried forward by your yin energy. The yin energy is characterized by fluidity, coolness, flexibility. It is curvilinear, more reactive than active. Again, notice your breathing, your places of tension where the yin energy seems to emanate from within your body. Notice, too, your interactions with others as they come into your path. Take your time with this; be inventive, expressive, explore the fullest range of your yin qualities. Half the universe is made by this energy, so don't skimp here.

Having moved about in yin fashion for about the same time as that you devoted to yang, relax, center, and allow the yin qualities to ebb and come to a neutral position.

If you are working with a group of more than three, the following extensions of this experience will further heighten awareness of your yin/yang dynamic proportions:

- Half the group move across the room in yin fashion, half in yang, interact with one another when you may chance to meet.
- Reverse roles.
- All but one yin, the rest yang. All but one yang.
- Males yin, while females yang. Reverse roles.
- In the course of moving, every once in a while make your body "freeze." Notice where in yourself you feel tension, power, vulnerability, balance, disorientation.

More can be done to explore the yin/yang energies by extending the movements into dance, extending the vocalizations into song or simple instrumental music. The point is to somaticize the Yin/Yang qualities so that your body "knows" the various degrees and locations and sensations of its yin and yang energy. An hour expended on this phase is not at all too much.

Phase 2. To create visual expressions of these same principles, select either the yin or the yang quality. Now that you have had all your senses involved in expressing this energy, recollect what those experiences were like for you in anticipation of creating a visual expression of these experiences. To initiate the image making, select a sheet of paper to work on. Hold it both horizontally and vertically to determine which direction is most suitable for this energy to be best expressed. Before marking the page, move your hands across the page, feeling the movement from your shoulders to your fingertips, in a fashion consistent with the way you experienced this particular energy flow. Notice the scope and direction of your movements, be aware of the pressure you are applying to the page. Use the whole page just as you used the entire room to move in. Notice what is occurring in your neck, chest, face as you work. Don't think as much as *notice.*

Now select a focused range of colors that feel appropriate for the expression of this energy. Hold the medium (brush, crayon, charcoal, etc.) in your hand in what you feel to be a yin or yang position. Now, with the yin (yang) energy flowing fully, mark the page with your medium. Allow your hand to do what it will, allowing your eye to acknowledge its path rather than to guide it. When the image has run its course, stop and spend a while surveying your handiwork. After an appropriate pause to allow that energy principle to fade, move through the same steps with its complement.

Once you have completed both, it will be instructive to put the two sheets side by side and again survey them. You may ask yourself the following questions as you do so:
- How do the various elements of line, form, texture, color, in the yin work differ from those used in the yang?
- How do the organizational principles (pattern, rhythm, dominance, etc.) differ in each?
- How did you feel as you made each one? Did you experience naturalness, ease, power?
- What emerged that you did not anticipate?
- What confirmed what you already knew?
- How are your yin and your yang imagery similar?
- Which seems, in sum, closer to the *you* that you know?

*Phase 3.*We are, of course, neither completely yin nor completely yang but a particular combination of both, and we spin our own way as a consequence of the dynamic tension created by these two complementary forces. As a final exercise we will employ both the yin and the yang energies in the creation of a work portraying the complex person we actually are.

Select a sheet of paper of a size and shape that you feel makes a suitable arena for the yin and yang forces to play out their hands. Once again begin either with the yin or the yang, working until the force's presence on the paper is assured. Then introduce the complementary element into the arena and allow it to run its course. Continue as you will, working alternately with yin and then yang. As the image takes form, be particularly attentive to the zones of interaction where yin dances close to yang. You may find that one hand is more yin than yang, while the reverse is true for your other hand. If so, try yanging with one hand, yinning with the other.

When the work has run its course, set it aside and perhaps take a break. Let your eyes rest and let the work simmer a bit without watching over it. After an appropriate time, come back to your work and once again look at it, slowly, carefully. As you do so, you may ask yourself the following questions:

- What is present in this work that did not appear in the two prior ones?
- What qualities have been retained?
- What qualities about yourself are more fully accounted for in this work?
- What differences are there in the quality of energy, in its subtlety, range, complexity, depth, scope?
- When yin and yang combine their mutual forces, is any hybrid vigor noticed?

After studying the work by yourself, you may gain additional insights by sharing your thinking with a partner. Such sharing, as we've seen elsewhere, can uncover certain elements that are more easily seen by an outsider. Also, speaking your mind to and in front of another tends to solidify and clarify your thinking, affirm your feelings.

We have for so long in our history and so deeply in our lives experienced the other gender as somehow alien, a polar opposite to our own gender. Perhaps the adversarial relations so often experienced between the genders are a projection of our own intrapsychic denial of the indwelling presence in us all of both masculine and feminine natures. Perhaps, too, this opposing-gender relationship is ready to give way to the more inclusive and life-affirming conception of the complementary relationships of masculine/feminine, anima/animus. The yin/yang encounter provides a stage of experiences on which that brave new world may be explored, and where creative energies now locked in futile battle may be released to our real advantage.

TO THE LAND OF PEACE AND WELL-BEING: GUIDED IMAGERY

Is there a person alive who cannot imagine a setting for his or her life that would distinctly improve upon the life that they have? Imagining such a land is no idle fantasy; indeed, we measure the pleasures of our life by comparing the products of our imagination against the life that we have. This imagined land is also the direction—however slanted or tortuous—in which we steer what we can of our lives.

The following exercise employs the capacity to imagine the look of our land of peace and well-being. It is a land that holds restorative qualities, a place all of our own, in which whatever is present is there solely by invitation of our imagination. Its creation begins in our mind's eye, according to whose vision physical images are created, eventually establishing them in the physical world. To help us journey to this imaginary land of peace and well-being, we will employ a process called guided imagery. This is a practice in which one travels mentally to times and places that are generated by acts of the imagination. It is like purposeful dreaming or deliberate day-dreaming, whereby your concentration focuses not on where you physically are, but on where your mind wanders. To follow a thought for more than a few moments, however, we first need to disengage as best we can with life as it impinges upon us moment by moment. Since this will initially be an inner excursion, the less the mind is called upon to react to information from the physical world, the more it can pay attention to creations of its own. A quiet, secure place, a comfortable position, a fair amount of discretionary time will help us to hoist our sails and sail free.

You can guide yourself on such a journey; it is far easier, however, if someone else guides you. Guiding yourself requires two mind-sets operating alternatingly: one with a plan, describing the next phase of the journey, the other following the map set by the guide and creating the particular landscape covered by that map. In a guided imaginary journey you soften your grip on the realities of the physical dimension of living. It's no easy thing to do, and it's always done with some perceived risk in taking your hands off the steering wheel while the vehicle of life hurtles forward. In this vulnerable situation, it is good to have a trustworthy companion nearby who is awake and vigilant to the world as it is, so that you may wander unfettered for a while in the direction of the world as you would have it.

Encounter

The following encounter is one version of a guided journey to the "land of peace and well-being." Many paths may lead to similar places, so shape it to your own ways and particular setting. To the degree that it provides a genuine experience for the person guiding the journey, to that same degree will it allow the sojourner to have an authentic and potentially rewarding experience.

Phase 1. In a relaxed posture, sitting or reclining in a quiet space, close your eyes and begin by just noticing your breathing rhythm. Don't do anything about it, just passively notice it, how it takes care of itself and takes care of you, naturally, easily, without your control. Notice, too, the ground underneath you, supporting you, making a snug fit between you and the world.

Be aware of yourself lying, here, aware of the clothes you are wearing, your hair, how you are wearing it today, the light playing on it. Be aware of yourself lying on the surface of the earth, breathing in, breathing out, naturally, automatically.

Imagine yourself now looking down at yourself from a height of the ceiling. There you are, you see your whole body in one glance, relaxed, quiet. If others are with you, you can see your companions nearby, you see their bodies, what they are wearing, how motionless they also are. Allow your eyes to pass over these figures, you and them resting comfortably there. Simply acknowledge what you see.

Imagine now that you are floating higher still, at the level of the treetops. You see yourself still lying beside your companions. You can still make out hair color and the color of clothing, but no longer can you recognize your distinctive features or theirs. You also see the shapes of your surroundings. The setting for this guided imagery is a room within a building in a town or city. At this height, the geometry of city life becomes apparent to you: angles of roofs, corners of buildings, lines of sidewalks. Growing things appear as bursts of different shades of color.

You float still higher, as high as the high-flying birds. Now the town beneath you appears as a geometric pattern: trees are small green dots, roads are gray lines, houses are patched rectangles, lawns, gardens, parks are green edging and swaths. People are tiny dark spots, vehicles are big, colorful rectangular blocks. The land is a marvelously complex quilt stretching out forever. Above it all is uninterrupted sky. As you look down from the heights, feel the breeze through your hair, feel the sun warming one side of your body, your other side cool and fresh.

Float higher still now into soft clouds. Benath you, clouds, white, pink, pale blue gossamer, above and around you the same. You float easily, marveling at the buoyancy of these puffs of white. The atmosphere here is somewhat cooler, the light more diffuse and iridescent. You breathe in the lightness and the enveloping mist, and it all feels good. You begin to become aware that there seems to be a direction to your floating, something quietly

but inexorably is pulling you in a particular way, and you allow that to happen, feeling yourself gently carried along by this gentle tide.

After some time, you notice a patch of blue ahead of you. It enlarges as you float toward it, a clear, washed blue, opening onto a view of the earth below. As you float toward the opening in the clouds you see the blue above and the green below, and you feel there is a faint but certain familiarity to this place and that it awaits you just as you are drawn to it.

Floating down closer to the ground, you feel even more at ease, a vague sense that you are returning home. You feel the warm sun on your face and the gentle wind against your skin. You breathe the passing aromas of a fruitful land. Slowly looking around, look deeply at this not-so-strange landscape. Let all that you see wash over you, soothe you.

Now, touch down lightly and feel the earth beneath you, hear the sounds your feet make as you tread the land. Touch the grasses that you walk through, their thin, cool, soft blades. Look to your right, then to your left, scanning the scope of this welcoming land. While on your sojourn you become aware that in the distance there is an indistinct figure, one whom you feel drawn to. Making your way across the land and moving in the direction of the figure, as you draw closer it becomes clear who this person is who awaits you. You approach closer still and, as you look knowingly at each other, the two of you embrace. It is now clear that this person is the one that loves you in ways so necessary for you to be loved. How full of wonder it is to hold and be held by your loved one. How reassuring the embrace. Look into each other's eyes, go over familiar features, allow your eyes to caress each line, shape, and texture of the face before you. Without words being spoken audibly, you say to each other what needs saying. And each of you understands.

After a while, it is clear that your loved one must leave, and so must you, each knowing that this will not be the last meeting or parting. You step back away from each other. You leave something of yourself, your loved one leaves something with you in turn. Still facing each other, you both recede from the place of encounter. You know that person is an essential part of your land of peace and well-being and that you will meet again.

Receding farther still, you feel yourself becoming lighter, and lighter still. Gravity has no hold on you now, and you begin to float away and up, the land becoming a blanket beneath you, the clouds once again enfolding you. Floating upward, the current gently lofts you, carrying you along on an unmistaken tide, a generous and inexorable wash. Giving yourself up to its pull, you sense you are being carried back to your other, temporal home.

As you float through the clouds you are also buoyed along by new emerging sensations of time, of love, of inner peace and well-being. Float easy, allow yourself to be carried along, pale blue above, soft green below, all veiled in the mist of your envelope of clouds. After being gently swept along for a while, you begin to feel yourself slowly descending, descending until once again you float free of the clouds and can see the land below. With a different but welcoming sense of recognition, you see what is also familiar to you: the land from where your journey began. There beneath you, at the level of the flying birds, is your town. Once again the lines for roads, the blocks for buildings, the dots for people. Your town.

Floating down farther still, at the level of the treetops, you see distinctly the buildings, windows, walkways, trees, and grass you know so well. You look at it all carefully, noticing that familiar tree, those angles. And there right beneath you is a group of people, your people, the companions of your way. And there you are. It *is* you, you recognize the colors and cut of your clothing, the color and sweep of your hair. Even though your features are just discernible, it most certainly is you.

Come down closer still, just above the ground, and look carefully at your face. Your eyes are closed, your mouth relaxed and soft, your skin glistening with life flowing beneath. Look at your hands, open, soft, waiting. You see yourself breathe, the rising and falling of your chest, as the air fans your inner fire.

Now reenter your own body, and experience your breathing from the inside. You can feel the air rush in and swell your chest. You feel the warmer air rush back out, making soft whooshing sounds. You inhale with greater vigor, purposely expanding your chest, allowing more air in, feeling your muscles stretch to make room for this new volume. You flare your nostrils, pushing the air out, hearing its exit.

Just as you stretched your chest, now stretch your arms, reaching out, flexing your waiting muscles. Feel the ground pressing against you, feel your hands, let your fingers touch the ground, know it again, touch your face. You are back, and you are well.

When you are ready, open your eyes, open your ears, open your mouth, and tune your equipment to this world as it is, right here and right now. You may feel somewhat disoriented, even vulnerable, as you just return. Take some time to regain your bearings. You might want to go for a walk by yourself to reacquaint yourself with your physical body and its sensations. Don't wander too far or long by yourself at this phase, because the subsequent phases of this exercise will help you to process and synthesize the thoughts and sensations you encountered, which still may be "out there" while you feel yourself to be back "in here." You may want to look into a full-length mirror for a while, to become acquainted with this traveler who just returned from a most important journey. You may wish to make contact with one of your companions, to just touch hands, embrace in a reassuring hug.

Phase 2. It has been a long journey, and much has transpired. In your own time, and by yourself, employing whatever medium feels appropriate, you are now invited to create an image expressive of that moment of your journey that struck the deepest resonances within you. This may be a particularly moving experience for you. The meeting with a special person, the speaking what needed to be said may raise extremely tender issues. Saying things to someone who resides now in our mind's eye, things that couldn't be said face-to-face on the physical plane, may tug deeply at our hearts. The making of a visual metaphor of the experience you just had now presents an opportunity to synthesize these still-raw emotions. Go slowly here, lean into your drawing, allow the strokes to absorb the impact of your feelings. Allow the activity of the drawing to be a soliloquy, as you once again plow that fertile ground of your encounter. The imaging ought not to be a waking illustration of what was completed during your guided imagery. If the work at hand is to have transformative powers, it, like your encounter, must be experienced as if for the first time.

When the work has run its course, take some time to look at it. Carefully. Running your eyes over what your hands have just made helps to deepen your associations with this land of peace and well-being, and with your loved one who resides there—with you and within you.

Processing

If you are working in the companionship of others, an effective way to process the created work and the related experiences is to select one or two companions and together share those aspects of your encounter and your work.

The following questions may be helpful in clarifying the worth of the experience:

- Where did you go? How did you feel there?
- What were the major features in your land of peace and well-being? How are those elements especially necessary or rewarding for you?
- What were your physical sensations upon arriving there? What emotional reactions did you experience, what thoughts occurred to you?
- Were there any surprises in relation to where you went, who you saw, what occurred?
- Looking at the image you made based on your journey and meeting, are any atypical elements present, such as new imagery, use of color, line quality, vitality of stroke, compositional devices, or the like?
- Was it easier for you to take off from where you are now to your far and distant land, or was it easier to return home? Why? How?

Extensions: If there are any new expressive elements in your work, they are well worth further exploration. Something in your guided-visualization experience may have opened a new domain of expression for you. Not simply did you journey to a novel territory, but your journey may have uncovered or unbound something of personal importance. It might be of value now to stay with these elements longer and explore their (your) further reaches. Focus on the elements that seem to catch at you the strongest, and once again allow your hand to find its way, reserving your eyes for acknowledgment.

147

This land to which you have traveled may be visited again whenever you wish. You know where it is and how to get there. You need only give yourself the gift of sufficient time and the permission of your imagination/memory, and you are there. Your friend will be there for you also, if you choose. Conjuring up places of the mind puts at our disposal a power to change a dimension of the world we inhabit, one which to a surprising degree compensates for some of the difficulties of the temporal, spatial, seemingly capricious world into which we were born and in which we can do less than we wish to. This act of deliberate imagination is very much a creative act, one that is both empowering and reassuring.

THE NUB OF YOU

There is an essential quality that each of us has, without which we would no longer be the person we are. It is this nub of ourself that we seek in the following encounter.

The person who we take ourselves to be is composed of myriad traits. The sum total of this constellation of particular qualities forms our sense of self. Some of these traits are of the moment, adopted when fashionable, dropped when not. Other traits run more deeply, resist time and most circumstances. At the core of these central attributes reside a select few that form the very core of our being. It is not easy to describe these core qualities because they are so infrequently called for. Also, they lie at the level of our deepest—and therefore unexamined—conceptions of reality. They predispose us to value what we do and to play out our hand in our own way. Manifesting themselves through more overt behavior, they themselves remain unnamed.

However deeply they may be hidden and how rarely seen as such, these core traits nonetheless provide the foundation or, better still, the matrix upon which our day-to-day contact with the world is assembled and given consistent form. Each day we create our sense of the world, and we do so by assembling our moment-to-moment sensations within a ready underlying personal cosmology. Gaining an insight into what lies at the center of our sense of self offers us the opportunity to examine the look of our primary self; raising this hidden core identity to the level of awareness allows us to assay its qualities if we choose to—the first step—and then to modify that which no longer serves us well. This is what we are after in seeking the nub of ourselves.

At the very core of us also resides a tremendous amount of energy, which when tapped may be employed in the exercise of imagination and creativity. It has often been observed that under extreme circumstances, when we have had stripped from us every protective device and mask, and danger threatens us or a loved one, our body taps a source of energy of uncommon magnitude. Strength, endurance, insight, compassion, are then present in surprising degree. This source of energy is what we are after now, so that we may employ these extraordinary forces to bear upon our creative endeavors.

There is another reason we seek this source. At this center, this nub of our being, lies a richness born of a sense of assuredness and ultimacy. When all the veneers of propriety have run their course and cleverness and pleasantries will no longer do, there remains a core of inner qualities, resistant, ancient and primal, yet in a surprising way childlike and new. These few qualities when uncovered have a fresh look and usually emerge with great verve.

149

That artist is decidedly advantaged who knows what this nub looks like, how it feels to be at its center, how to get there, and how to employ these energies for creative enterprises.

Encounter

The exercise itself is simple enough. Before setting out to do anything, pause for a while and meditate on the phrase "The Nub of Me." You needn't have an image in mind as a result of this. It is better, in fact, that you do not. Focus your attention simply on that phrase, "The Nub of Me." Don't rush this meditation; let it percolate through your mind-body, coursing along all your channels and byways. After a sufficient while, go about gathering any media that feel appropriate to investigate this nub of you. As you pass before your eyes and hands the variety of options open to you—clay, paint, pastel, wood—some will feel more appropriate in your hands than others. You know when something feels right in your hand and you know when it doesn't.

Once you have provided yourself with the initial media through which you will investigate this region of the core of you, begin to form the thing that seems to emerge. Again, don't try to determine the meaning of the piece as it takes form, or be too heavy-handed in your early assessments of its worth and—especially—of its craft. Let the knowledge that resides in the deep musculature of your frame guide your hands. Your eyes at this phase of the experience are to be used just to acknowledge the presence of your hand at work. Let the piece go where it will, allow yourself to continue working even though there might be periods of confusion, surprise, chagrin, amazement. Uncover, recover, discover.

Processing

When your journey toward the nub of you has run its course, and you sense there is sufficient fullness and depth to the image, stop. Now, by yourself, look at it carefully, becoming acquainted with what you see and what you are feeling as you contemplate its just-emerged presence.

The following questions may help guide you in your reflections:
- As you now look at your work, recount the process you experienced in uncovering this central dimension of yourself. What seemed like break-through images, colors, or gestures? What resistances did you encounter that you were required to push on through?
- What were your somatic reactions as you came upon and overcame these veils obscuring, then revealing, your core self?

150

- How do you now name what you now see of your inner self?
- Is this a relatively new you that you see, or does it have deep roots in your personal history, the history of your family?
- What about this work looks/feels familiar? What looks strange and new?
- What is the character of the energy in the work, the character of this power? What kind of strength is exhibited here?

This is a useful encounter to process with others—not to have them interpret for you what they see, but to have them *describe* what they see and what they experience upon seeing your work. Often the imagery and style of this work is novel to such a degree that there is difficulty for its author to take cognizance of what is there. Those who have less vested interest in the image and who are not involved with its process of creation often have an easier time discerning important elements that are actually there but remain veiled to its author. So do, if you are working in the company of others, share your reflections, use one another to heighten and deepen the original experience. As always when speaking to others about their art, be mindful of speaking of only what you experience as a consequence of witnessing the piece and don't presume to know the mind of someone else.

Extensions. You may extend the graphic and symbolic material uncovered during the creation of this work by taking those elements that seem new and evocative to you and going on to create other works featuring these elements. You may find that as you employ the imagery, the elements, and the energy elicited in this experience your work is likely to become richer and more evocative, the flow of expression more natural and personal.

JANUS MASKS

To every day there is a corresponding night; every light casts a shadow. Just so, there is a dimension of ourselves that we share with the everyday people of our lives, and there is another dimension of our being that we share, when we share it at all, with only a very special few. This "shadow" self runs deeper and is more central, more precious, and, we believe, more vulnerable than the face we show in public. In the following encounter we will be working with the energies we use to keep this face in the shadow, in the hopes of reallocating those same energies for more rewarding purposes.

It is only right to protect what is most valuable. But the enormous amount of energy we devote to this effort of concealment is diverted from the pool of energy available to us for other things, particularly for creative experiences. We put so much time into building and defending our barricades that little time or resources remain to celebrate what we are so busy defending. A pity. The things that are so dear and so central about ourselves rarely see the light of day. The things we keep from others we necessarily have to keep from ourselves. The things about ourselves that might be used to join us with others, to create a quality of relating to the world, we keep hidden in darkness and silence. For whom and for what are we preserving these precious qualities?

It is not at all difficult to understand why we exact such a price from our life. The reasoning is that if we do expose the most precious quality of ourselves, and it is undervalued or rejected, then we will indeed be cut to the quick and will have no further reserve of well-being to fall back upon.

But perhaps our fears are exaggerated. It may just be that when we do uncover and share our cherished qualities, that in the brave and vulnerable act of doing so we encourage the development of a more caring and attentive partner. It is important here to recognize that no one is altogether dumb and foolish. Even the most dull and armored know a brave and deep gesture from a shallow one. My experience has always been that as I go deeper within myself and share significant portions of my self-discoveries with my partner, my partner reciprocates. If I'm facile and chatty, my companions will be too. If I've offered something tender and dear in either word or tone, something that meets their own vocabulary of responses, they will be there for me.

Encounter

This exercise is about finding ways to uncover the shadowed and precious self and in a safe context share that precious aspect with others. The gain for this effort may well be the release of a great deal of creative energy and imagination now locked into defensive masking.

A Note on Masks. Masks are employed in this exercise because masks, with their uncanny powers as transformative devices, will serve us well in this delicate matter of uncovering (unmasking) our shadow self. There is something about a mask that reveals and conceals at the same moment. Masks trick the viewer into being moved by the presence residing beneath the surface of the mask, even as that same viewer knows that it is only a facade of wood, paper, or tin. The same thing happens to the wearer of the mask; knowing full well that he or she remains intact behind the mask, the wearer nonetheless takes on attributes of the mask that are most difficult to reach without it. Why is there no power in the mask unless it is worn—and seen—by humans? How does the mask live—or remain a dead thing? Questions for other times and circumstances. For now it is sufficient to point to the power of a veil. Or lipstick!

Phase 1. Consider the public aspect of you, the face you put on for your usual public. This facade has stood you in good stead with those you need to impress, those relationships that are bounded by status, propriety, deference. This is the pleasant face you turn to the world, one which shows you are a decent sort, likeable and trustworthy. It's the face (mask) you employ with casual acquaintances, neighbors, business associates, and at family functions. . . . You know. When this general sense of yourself is in focus, begin to create a mask that represents this "face." Do make the mask large enough so that you can wear it. Any media will do for the mask: paper bags, newspaper, cardboard, fabrics, paints, string. Once again, allow your imagination free rein in your selection of materials, fitting your choices to the aims that you intend.

When the mask is completed, set it aside for the moment.

Phase 2. Following the making of this public mask, reflect upon that "other" dimension of yourself. This aspect of you runs deeper, is more central and more substantive. Because it is so precious, it may well be a particularly vulnerable characteristic. If this is undervalued by others, then the very essence of your being, your sense of dignity, may be denied. Again, spend the necessary time to secure the appropriate media and permit yourself to fashion an image that is fully expressive of this rarely emergent, but absolutely essential, shadow self.

Phase 3. When both masks are completed, take them both and, selecting a partner (who also has completed two masks), find a place where the two of you have a fair degree of auditory privacy. You need not be very picky about

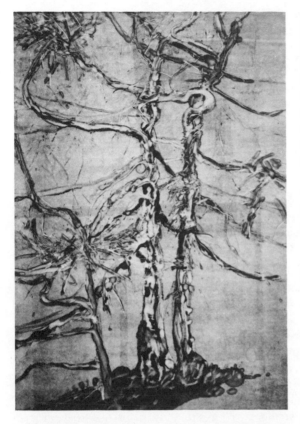

your partner because his or her role will be silently supportive rather than interactive. Then sit facing each other, close enough for a conversation. You put on the shadow mask, your partner puts on *your* public mask. Your partner is to *remain silent* while wearing your mask, but may silently gesture to support your talk.

Wearing your shadow mask, and looking at your public mask, speak to that public facade. Speak about what comes to your mind and heart when *you* see your public mask. Speak of what you feel when you see this persona. Speak of the price of public acceptability, the power it affords you, the hurts and uncertainties it masks. Speak your mind and heart. Allow this session sufficient time for a full expression of sentiment. (Too much time spent at this, however, may lead to defensive chatting. Perhaps fifteen minutes will serve best for our purposes.)

Once you've said what needed saying to your public facade, have your partner take that mask off and put on the mask of your shadow self. Wait a moment; look long at this face before speaking. Give this stage sufficient time. When you have scrutinized this shadow dimension of you and felt its presence in your life, then say what needs saying to this face. You will know what must be said; often it just emerges with an urgency that is surprising. Remember, your partner best serves your coming to terms with both dimensions of yourself by bearing *silent* witness to you facing yourself. The less intrusive your partner is, the more candid and full your own expressions can be. Speaking to these two primary dimensions of our being, speaking out loud and in a semipublic forum often elicits strong emotions and touches upon primary material. As a consequence, when you have completed your dialogues with both your public and shadow selves, you may need some time to synthesize the experience. Take as long as you need. You may need silence, or you may need the supportive companionship of your partner. Before moving on to the next phase of this experience (in which you exchange roles), do center yourself, allowing the new experiences to slowly assimilate into your system.

Now exchange roles. As you wear your partner's public and shadow face in turn, attentively witness your partner's coming to terms with both dimensions of himself or herself.

Processing

Experience with the dynamic of this encounter has proved it to be very powerful and moving. It is no easy thing to face yourself and to finally say what has been denied or repressed for a long time. Certainly one such transaction does not release all that there is to say and to confront, nor is this single encounter intended to do any such thing. But speaking frankly and fully about any issue of importance is an emotional experience, both emotionally draining and subsequently energizing. We do want art experiences that make a difference in our lives. This encounter invites the possibility of substantial growth, and if it is undertaken with a desire on our part to evolve, there is the strong likelihood that long-ossified emotional and creative energies will be released, resulting in a noticeably lighter being, a new exuberance for living in its expansive possibilities.

As a consequence of releasing one's confining grasp on critical and personal identities, there may very well follow a period of emotional tenderness and a surfeit of yet unallocated energy. It is important therefore to remain in a supportive, caring space for a while with your partner as you begin to adjust to your new sense of self. Having borne silent witness to each other, having exposed and shared qualities rarely acknowledged before, you and your partner can continue to support and affirm each other by sharing further, this time in open—unmasked—conversation. Be generous with the time you give to this, and allow the exchange to run its full course. Here is a rare opportunity to experience support and to offer your support in return. This is an opportunity to allow yourself to come close to an "other," to touch the world in a new place and, as a consequence of your "unmasking," in a new way.

Subsequent Activities. Having experienced the encounter with your shadow self and brought it newly to the light, it will be good to build up this newly emergent self more fully in the world. You may further explore and solidify your new self-perceptions by now creating an image expressive of the experiences you just had addressing your public and your shadow self. What did you experience when you saw these aspects of yourself? What was it like for you to say what you did? You might now create a metaphoric image embodying the confrontation with your facades.

The other significantly moving dimension of this experience involves your reactions to witnessing your partner's confrontations with his or her masks. You were there, privy to rarely exposed and very central material. How was it for you to receive that, to be in some indistinct way responsible to hold that information in trust? You may find your emotions clarified by creating an image of what you experienced of your partners' coming to terms with themselves. You may then work again with your partner, sharing your separate and mutual works and reactions.

You may also approach this general encounter under a number of other circumstances. Instead of creating the dynamic between your shadow and public selves, you might deal with other complementarities, such as the yin and yang of you, the poet and the pedestrian of you, the body and the spirit of you.

Because the Janus Masks encounter can be very evocative, you may desire a period of time to assimilate the meanings and feelings it has evoked. This is a good time for a long walk with a trusted companion, perhaps not to talk, just a side-by-side walk. The reconciliation of these two dimensions of your self has most likely not run its course in such a short time, but you have made a beginning. Do allow this more resolved and vitalized self to become further actualized through subsequent creative endeavors. Be sure to give yourself the time and space to let this happen. Another painting, a poem?

EDEN LOST AND REGAINED

It may be everyone's ambition at some point to dwell in the garden of Eden, the place that contains the fleeting glimpses we occasionally have of "the good life." This theme of uninterrupted bliss appears in many cosmologies, in many peoples' mythic descriptions of the world, and to some degree it animates every life. We all head to our own Eden as best we can, encumbered as we may be by our inherited world, body, and mind. Finding the means to portray the major features of our Eden is a task that offers many rewards, not the least of which is a declaration and celebration of how we would ultimately prefer to live.

We all head for Eden, meaning that we steer our lives as best we can to meet our own conception of well-being. Of course our bearings are inaccurate, our craft somewhat faulty, and our map at best uncertain. That's life. Nonetheless, the choices we make in life, when we have the presence of mind to choose, are informed in real measure by our vision of Eden.

To portray our garden of Eden is to portray the values we live by and the goals we seek. It is an important engagement with that which animates the major features of our life, and when taken up fully, it offers a revealing vision of the net worth of our living.

Just as the myths, religions, cosmologies, and personal histories of the world's societies often contain an unspoiled, pristine garden of Eden (as in the Jewish, Christian, and Islamic religions), they also contain an episode of an expulsion or fall from that earthly Paradise. I know of no society that holds that we are presently dwelling in the original Eden. Some transgression, some defect in the human psyche caused us to be expelled from this original and infinite bliss.

Once (they tell us) we had it all, then (so they say) we defaulted, and now we are separated from what we had, which was all good. Each mythic tradition describes why mankind was expelled from its Eden and parted us from our original unity, purity, and bliss. The particular reason for the expulsion coincides with what each particular society holds as most precious. In the case of Christians, Jews, and Muslims the mythic story tells of our being expelled from the Garden of Eden because we did eat of the one fruit barred to us, the fruit of the knowledge of good and evil. Much has been written of this transgression and what it implies about God, man, woman, reason, sin, nature, good, evil—in short, about all the conceptions that make up our sense of what is proper in the world and our appropriate place in it.

The creative process is always marked by charting new territory, leaving behind what we know, following uncertain paths, working with what we have, accommodating ourselves to the world as it is and hoping that the next time will be a better time. The encounter I call Eden Lost and Regained calls upon these same abilities, tests their vigor, examines their boundaries, and offers the chance to extend those boundaries. When we are in the very midst of a thing it is all but impossible to notice its boundaries, where it lets off and something else takes over. In this same way we must leave our Eden to know what we had. Just as death gives life its cherished values, so does the expulsion from Eden give Paradise its value.

The creation of our Eden, the loss of this same Eden, and the return to a "weathered" Eden is as provocative an experience as it is an ultimately rewarding one. This journey tests one's mettle in many ways. And in just those same ways it can open the doors of perception. That, of course, is our goal.

In this exercise we are first in, then outside of our Eden, the better to comprehend and cherish where we were and where we are heading. Finally, having surveyed the Eden we chose, then left it to better appreciate where we were, we can further explore the meanings that reside here by subsequently returning to the Eden that we were forced to leave, making it once again our own.

Encounter

This particular encounter requires that there be a group of at least three people (and preferably more). You can practice elements of this encounter by yourself, but its full reward derives from the interaction of several people and their efforts at creating, leaving, and reclaiming their garden of Eden.

Phase 1. The image of your garden of Eden may be arrived at via any one of a number of means. For example, you may visualize your garden through a guided-imagery process and then illustrate what you encountered in your mind's eye. You can meditate for a while on the phrase "my garden of Eden" and then directly create a visual metaphor expressive of that interior experience. Or with no preliminaries you may just launch right into the activity, brush and paint in hand, allowing your hand and heart to find their way into your garden. In this way you discover your Eden as you go along. Whatever your means, all paths will lead to the same place.

Now to begin. On a rather large sheet of paper—say, four by three feet—using any medium you deem appropriate, create an image of your garden of Eden. Interpret that invitation any way you wish: it's your Eden.

Phase 2. When work has progressed to a point where the major features are presented *but are still in the main incomplete,* interrupt your work.

Set your tools down and leave them where they are. You are being asked now to leave your just-begun Eden, not because of any fault of your own, but because life is like this: full of undertakings curtailed by outside forces.

The weave of life is tight, but the pattern does not begin or end with us. Things happen. It is time for you to leave your Eden. Take a long breath and, with one last glance at your garden-in-the-making, bid it farewell and launch into the deep. You most likely will find this hard to do—to leave off the creation of your Eden before it is completed and before you have had the opportunity to savour its rewards. The pride of ownership of the first garden, the one created in pristine conditions, has no counterpart in any subsequent efforts we may make in already tilled land. It *is* difficult—just like life. Now wander among the other gardens left vacant by their owners. Notice, too, how their dreams are similarly unfulfilled, their plans unrealized. As you walk through these other Edens, try to find one (not your own) that nonetheless feels congenial. When you do, enter it, settle there, and make it your own. Use the previous owner's abandoned tools to create your new garden of Eden.

Just as in life, good things slip away from us. Things not of our wishing fall apart. In some fashion we are all nomads, forced again and again to break camp and to follow yet another star, find another place, work to make that place a home. We are always in the midst of our becoming, our planning and hopes for a better future to come. Be careful as you go about claiming this garden as your own, making this new Eden conform to your own conception of the good and the beautiful. You have inherited something of value. In this garden reside aspirations and visions culled from a lifetime. Find a balance between your respect for what has been given to you and your own claims to imagination and personal values. Dare to be both respectful and true to yourself.

Phase 3. After a while, perhaps fifteen minutes, having worked on this inherited garden and having begun to make it your own, once again cease your efforts and lay down your tools. Once again you are asked to leave this garden too soon to have completed your vision but having had enough time to begin to shape it in your preferred way. Once again you are asked to wander about, to seek still another abandoned garden to claim and make your own. The second exile most likely will be different from the first. You may find that your new efforts to create a garden of Eden on the foundations of some secondhand Eden are dispirited and without hope. Or you may take courage from these forced leavetakings, vesting your enthusiasm in the process of creation and not in the value of what that process manifests. How you perceive these exiles and enterings will determine to a large degree the kind of Eden you create and the emotional climate within that garden.

Repeat this process—entering someone else's garden, claiming it as your own, respectful of your inheritance but authentically yourself—two or three more times.

Phase 4. Finally, after this long absence and its repeated sequence of loss, wandering, building, loss, and inheritance, return to your original garden of Eden. Before you do so, collect your bearings and prepare yourself for your return. You know that you left your own Eden before you had completed its design; certainly you left not on your own volition. Then strangers entered your garden, unbidden and unknown to you. They dwelt there a while, just as you dwelt in their gardens uninvited. They were allowed to claim your Eden as their own, just as you claimed theirs. Again and again each of you was forced to leave, forced to make over your inheritance to your liking.

Much has therefore transpired. Your original garden has been occupied and made over by many strangers. Thoughtful and careful as they may have been, they could not know your plans for Eden. Much then may be unfamiliar; perhaps the barest foundations remain of your original dream. Reclaiming what was yours may be not at all easy, but it is well worth trying. The task now is to find a way to reenter your dream of Eden, covered over as it may be with other dreams and ways, and to once again make it your own. Do what you will to make this your own. In life, this is a life's work. Under these artificial, condensed circumstances accord your creation a dignified amount of time, an hour, a morning, the day.

Upon completion of this final episode of the journey from Eden to Edens back to your own Eden, feelings have been tested; faith, trust, persistence have been called upon to the fullest. You have essentially worked alone in the course of this complex and demanding journey. Although you were a solitary worker, the poignancy and internal drama of that journey were created in large measure by the presence of others. You left your work to be continued by them, just as they left their work for you. You were constantly engaging in dialogue with others, even if obliquely and through their symbols and marks. Now it is time for you to meet face-to-face and share what has been privately thought and felt.

Processing

The following questions may help you to examine your experiences, clarify your perceptions, and solidify the gains you may have achieved through this series of encounters:

- What feelings were evoked as a consequence of having to leave your garden of Eden before it was completed?
- How did it feel, and what thoughts did you have, knowing that others came into your garden and made it over on their own terms?
- How was it for you to enter someone else's domain, occupy it, and attempt to make it your own?

- When asked to leave again and again, was it different for you each subsequent time? How and why?
- What did you experience when invited to return to your original, long-forsaken garden?
- What were your initial reactions to seeing what was left of your original garden and what had been added since your departure?
- What resources did you bring to bear on the task of recreating your new garden of Eden?
- What changes occurred in your thinking about your original garden that were acquired through your subsequent experiences?
- As you share your reactions with others and listen to theirs, how were your reactions unique? What did you share in common?
- What did you notice of the particular way you employed your time, space, color, elements to create, re-create, enter, and leave your gardens of Eden?

These series of encounters with your dream of Eden and your attempts to create it out of whole cloth and then out of the fragments of other dreams given to you creates a complex and dense web of experiences, one that most likely evokes conflicting feelings and new perceptions. Allow time now to let this welter of experiences simmer. Don't rush too quickly to judgments and conclusions. Just let it all steep. Acknowledge your sensations, take cognizance of the thoughts that seem to well up from deep inside. In some ways you have become new, and equally, you have tapped very ancient sources. Glory in this realization and allow it to find its way into the quality of your next works.

RANDOM ACTS OF KINDNESS, SENSELESS GIFTS OF BEAUTY

All too often we experience the legacy of our lives as falling far short of what we believe is only just and fair. At the same time, there are always others who, through no particular talent of their own, receive more than they deserve. With this mind-set in place, we feel in general cheated by life, our efforts going unrecognized and unrewarded. Probably we are right. We often do get less than we desire, and lousy things do happen to nice people. If we are generally inclined to see the world through this mind-set, we cannot help but to expend a significant portion of our available energy in feeling cramped, abused, abandoned, and bitter about a world that is so much less than it could be, so much more painful than it need be. Our imagination, expressiveness, creativity are all put to the service of self-consuming anger, disappointment, and jealousy. We feel self-righteous in these reactions; after all, bad things do happen to good people, and not enough bad things happen to bad people. Would it have been such a big deal for God to have made this a just universe? With a bit more effort this world could have been not only the incomprehensibly beautiful place that it is, it also could have been fair, something it certainly is not.

There are ways to remain indignant when fairness and justice are denied to ourselves and to others without paying the price of consuming our creative energies in paralyzing pain or despair. Just as there is a degree of senseless pain and injustice in our lives, so also are there senseless gifts of beauty and random acts of kindness.

It is to these gifts and acts that we now turn. It is confounding that the worst no-good scoundrel and the most blessed saint alike are permitted to see the same sunsets and snowfalls and hear the identical birdsong. But isn't it equally worth noting that even at the end of a foul day, in which we have acted like a cur, we are still presented with stars and moonlight as our undeserved dessert? We did nothing to deserve, could do nothing for or against even such commonplace gifts such as sunrises, snowfall, hearing, imagination, memory, springtime, eyesight, desire, nectarines, sleep, language, fingers, feelings, pizza, baby anythings, big other things. Is *this* fair, is this just? As much as we are denied, are we not also showered with gifts completely beyond our particular merits? If there is necessary room in our life for the expression of indignation, should there not be, if justice and fairness is our concern, time also for celebration and howling over our staggering good fortune?

Put still another way, as the justly acclaimed author Maya Angelou said at a talk not long ago at my university, "Don't forget to say thank you." She told first a story of her childhood, which was full to overflowing with its share of abuse and terror. She then went on to describe how she was also the beneficiary of countless acts of kindness, how not all of her spirit and genius went unnoticed by members of her family. Further on in her talk she mentioned authors and artists whose work had inspired her, shaped her thinking, broadened her vision of the world and its possibilities. None of these authors wrote with her particular welfare in mind. Nonetheless, her well-being had prospered on account of their efforts. Blind acts of giving, random philanthropy. However can we repay these debts? There are many possible ways, not the least of which is by saying, "Thank you." Writing a note: "Dear Mr. Baldwin, Thank you."

The effort needn't be elaborate; acknowledging is all. Acknowledging that our lives are shot through with senseless gifts of beauty, random acts of kindness binds us to these gifts and acts and makes them our own. They may come our way unaddressed, but by our act of acknowledging them, we enter into an active relation with them; not claiming that they came our way in return for our efforts, but claiming them simply as recipients of unconditional gifts in a world that from time to time works that way too.

It may be that, just to the degree that you experience life as an abundance of anonymous gifts, only to that same degree will you be able to give freely of your gifts. Much creative potential is freed up in this manner, energy that can flower with surprising abundance.

Encounter

Take some time now to take account of the people and events in your life that have rewarded you not because you worked to deserve them, but because they came to you as random acts of kindness, senseless gifts of beauty.

Phase 1. Meditate on these phrases: "random acts of kindness, senseless gifts of beauty." Images and words will inexorably emerge. And now, on a large surface, begin to write the names of these gifts and acts. Allow your hand to write where and how it will without much thought. Central events and people will probably surface rapidly, presenting you with items you may have thought mattered little, but that now on inspection seem to have shaped your life decidedly. After writing the key words, pause and read them over, allowing your eyes to rest on each word and silently, in some fashion, acknowledging their place in your life.

Phase 2. This done, the next phase of your encounter with this elaborate "thank-you note" is to infuse color into the tapestry composed of words, transforming word into image. Choose colors that best represent your associations with the things named. Allow the weave and pattern of your colors also to reflect your relations with those named. Carry this forward until you feel there is an appropriate expressive balance between the names and the images. This phase will probably require a good deal more time than the initial one, so allow for it.

Processing

At some point the enterprise will run its course. The page will feel full, ripe with love and thanksgiving. Emotions may very well run equally full. It might seem at first that this would be an appropriate time to withdraw to a private place and time and meditate on what has just transpired. But my experience has been quite the opposite: it is in fact particularly useful to process the results of the encounter in the company of others. Giving actual voice to what you love and declaring what you are thankful for in the presence of others further binds you to these others and affirms your appreciation of your relationship. So share with others what others have given to you: speak fully of the stirrings of your heart, set to stir by the gifts and beauty of others. And listening to others speak about the gifts that are dear to them can uncover further reasons for you to feel gifted and appreciative.

Extension. As a subsequent exercise, take the basic colors you employed in the just completed work and—leaving aside the words and the particular qualities that they represent—create a new work to celebrate the general mood of these gifts in your life. Allow the colors and the rhythms of your strokes to be the primary elements in this new work, permitting them to find their own appropriate shapes and composition. In this way you will move beyond the sensibility of indebtedness that informed your prior work to one of sheer outward-moving celebration. This celebration is now of you, the you who is the blossoming, the culmination of billions of improbable gifts from myriad nameless sources. An appreciation of this cannot help but lead to the quiet, sure desire to pass these gifts on. Despite the madness and cheapness of much of our lives, is not this desire to share with others our own gifts the fuel that drives our creative spirit forward?

BECOMING NEW

We are always in the process of becoming new, but because our minds are more facile at exercising memory than imagination, we fail to recognize this evolutionary quality of our life. Each morning upon rising we remember the person we were yesterday and form ourself in this new day more or less along the lines of the way we were. We do this, even though the person we were is not always the person we prefer ourselves to be. Memory requires merely dogged constancy. Imagination, by contrast, takes courage and confidence in the rightness of our creations; hence its rarity.

We also believe that there is an inexorable momentum to our lives over which we have little control. The universe is big, and we are small. We didn't make the life we have, life did this to us. In fact, much of life as it is does derive from life as it was and must be. But not all. The following encounter is about choosing to be new, choosing to be the person you prefer to be in spite of the ocean of history within which we all must swim. It is also about letting go of those elements of the person we are, but that we are ready now to lay aside.

There are occasions when we grow by holding on to what we have and layering it over with new material. When large changes are desired, however, we must often first give up some portion of what we have in order to make sufficient room for this new quality that we desire in our lives. Discarding old ways is, as we all know, difficult. After all, it is not just putting something aside; it is bracketing it somehow in our past. We don't acquire traits capriciously, and most likely we acquired the traits we do have because at one time that quality fit the person we felt we needed to be. It served us well in its time, but now times and our desires have evolved. Perhaps it is time now to set a particular trait aside and seek a better way. Yet because there are emotional and intellectual ties to this trait, we cannot simply wish it away. We have to use the energy with which we have held onto this trait, and reemploy that energy into relinquishing our hold and adopting the new quality we desire.

Encounter

"Becoming new" is composed of two essential creative endeavors, followed by a ritualized series of events that promote the ability to move from one phase of life toward another, preferred one.

Phase 1. The first phase asks you to consider a particular trait that you are ready now to discard, a trait that perhaps served you well in its day but is

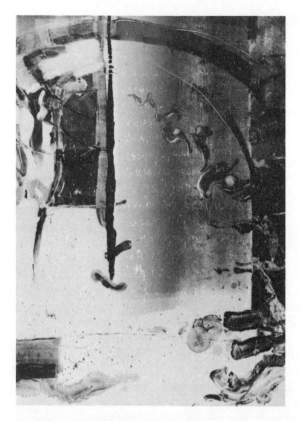

now no longer needed or desired. Using whatever medium seems appropriate, create a visual metaphor for this trait. You may want to include words with your images, combine found objects with ones of your own making. Once it is completed, spend a while by yourself looking at it, reviewing your association with it and your present feelings about discarding it. When your reflection has run its course, set this work aside for a while; we will employ it later as a part of a more inclusive experience.

Phase 2. Turn your attention now to a characteristic you desire for yourself. This may be a trait that is all but fully emerged right now, or it may be a quality that you eventually wish to acquire. The expectation is not that at the conclusion of this exercise you will have miraculously discarded an undesirable trait in your life and acquired a trait you find desirable. Life is not this facile, and neither is art. However, our desires do help to steer a course toward preferred destinations. Although we but infrequently achieve the goals we set out for, in the myriad choices we make each day we *can* make these choices in the direction of our desires. And so we can navigate, obliquely discovering, uncovering, recovering our way to a preferred life. Knowing the point from which we wish to depart and knowing our ultimate destination cannot help but inform our path. (Surely the absence of such knowledge can only lead to more uncertain places and attendant anxieties!)

So let us return to our next encounter: the defining of the person we prefer to be. Here again you can plunge right in and discover the parameters of this desired self as you go along or you can meditate on this for a while, focusing your mind, clarifying your thoughts before you actually lay hand to paper. As always, don't *illustrate* what is already created in your mind's eye; that would relegate the hand to the role of *slave* to the mind. Here, a partnership is far more desirable. Now, employing the medium you deem appropriate, go about creating a visual metaphor to portray this self that you seek to become.

Phase 3. The Ritual: You now have created two works. One represents a current personal quality that may have served you well before, but that now seems to serve more as an impediment to your becoming the person you wish to be. The other work represents the trait you wish to have more of in your life. The first phase of the transformational process will be to discard the undesirable item, the second will be to affirm the nature of the desired trait.

A number of sample ritualized processes designed to accomplish this end are listed below. Each one takes advantage of the unique context and participants for the particular design of the ritual. In a setting in the country, near a stream and waterfall, the participants were invited to gather around the top of the falls. One by one, each was asked to describe the quality they were ready to discard, how it had served them well in the past but how they were now ready to be rid of it. Having said what needed saying and in a style appropriate to the speaker, each person ceremoniously threw (placed gently, dropped) his or her work into the falls and watched it tumble out of sight, while the group cheered.

This affirming of desired qualities was animated by inviting the participants to form a tight circle. Each person was then asked to speak about the work representing the quality he or she wanted more of in life. After speaking, each person placed the object in the center of the circle. When all had said their piece, each person was invited to take a work home with them (*not* their own) and to hold onto it for a year. On the anniversary of this day they were asked to mail (or give) the work back to the original artist. The group did this as a reminder and confirmation of each artist's inner pledge to choose what they will to become the person they prefer themselves to be. Knowing that someone else has custody of our "pledge" and will be redeeming it has the effect of gently supporting our own convictions.

In another form of the ritual, held in a studio, classroom, or domestic setting, the participants were requested to gather in a circle, again with the works representative of the qualities they were ready to discard. Here again, they all spoke of what that trait was and how it had served them at another time and place but was now no longer desired. As each one spoke, he or she was invited to "deconstruct" that piece (by shredding, crumbling, folding, etc.) and to scatter its remains within the circle. When all the participants had spoken and shredded and scattered their work in the growing pile in the center of the circle, the pieces were swept together and placed in an elaborately decorated box. The group was then asked how best to dispose of this reverse Pandora's box. Once the decision was made—usually as a result of rather raucous deliberations—the box was ceremoniously discarded, by being buried, burned, dropped into the sea, floated out to sea, left on top of a mountain, hoisted to the top of a tree, whatever the local landscape, the talents of the group, and the neighbors could bear.

That quality we wished more of in our lives was then addressed. In this ritual the created metaphor for this desired quality was made in sufficient quantity for there to be one for each member of the group. Again forming a circle, the participants took turns speaking of the meaning represented by their work, that is, what trait each person wanted more of in life and was now prepared to seek. Describing how his or her piece represented that choice, the artist distributed to each other member of the group an example of that metaphor, a gestural painting, a brief poem, a clay figure, or the like. As the artist whose turn it was went around to the other participants, they were invited to indicate their appreciation for that particular person's help or companionship during the process of working together. This was a time for personal acknowledgment of our thanks, and at the same time this one-to-one expression of thanks was another way of confirming our decision to carry out what we had proposed. As a result of this circle of giving and receiving, we helped ourselves and one another to affirm our resolution to actually live in the direction of our desires.

Does this ritual of discarding the undesirable and affirming aspirations trivialize the actual difficulties involved in willfully changing the course of our life? I don't believe so. The experience released by this encounter is an engagement with big things, a necessary first step to raising important issues from an unnameable and unmanageable background to a deliberate foreground. The encounters were designed in such a manner that once having become the object of our attention, they fostered decisiveness in addressing them. Once we had privately determined our choices regarding what to let go and what to embrace, the choices made were then publicly spoken of. This last phase of the ritualized experience does what any public avowal does: by placing a private resolve within the public mind, we strengthen our resolve to get on with it—in this case, to get on with creating the life we prefer. Does one automatically follow from the other? Of course not. But it does help.

5

Media

NOT ART SUPPLIES—MEDIA

In the preceding sections, I have attempted to portray an expanded view of the domains of art and alternative ways to identify ourselves as artists. Now let us turn to the physical materials through which our minds may become manifest: the materials of artists. Here again, our prevailing conceptions of what art media are and what they do will need a thorough rethinking.

To most of us, the term *art supplies* connotes canvas, brushes, paint, and all the other things found in art stores. All the stuff we struggle mightily to tame and force to behave the way we wish. We can begin to expand its meaning simply by dropping that term and substituting the word *media*. *Media* is a more inclusive term, and in its meaning reside vaster and more powerful domains. The word *medium* derives from the Latin *medius,* meaning "middle." Media are things that stand between, in the middle of other things. This meaning nicely describes their function in the arts. Media are those things that stand between imagination and expression, between the mind and the act, the hand and the canvas. Media shuttle between the realm of thought and feeling and the concrete world of things and events. Media are the stuff that permit will to become manifest. *Art supplies* are often considered passive, inanimate things devoid of an inner vitality, blocks, dumb things. *Media* speaks of movement, of position and of transition.

Media are sometimes perceived as things that artists contend with in order to express their inner state of affairs. Frequently, there is an adversarial relation between the will of the artist and the medium that stubbornly resists that will. Art materials then become things that must be overcome, mastered. A great deal of time and frustrated effort is spent in forcing the uncooperative material to do what we wish. We want yielding and compliant material to do our bidding!

If they are thought of in this way, we keep our media as the "other," something that we control, something with no spirit or will of its own, yet something that resists our mind and will. With much practice, according to this notion, the elusive qualities of the media are overcome and our superior skill and patience prevail. We make an "it" of our instruments rather than work in harmony with them. We place our energy in the service of struggle rather than in cooperative interaction.

Martin Buber, in *I and Thou,* describes the act of creating an abiding relationship between ourselves and the full self of another. Of course he is speaking of the dialogue between human and human and that between humankind and God. But we can transpose this same quality of relationship to refer to that between the artist and his or her media.

> If I face a human being as my *Thou,* and say the primary word *I–Thou* to him, he is not a thing among things, and does not consist of things.
>
> This human being is not *He* or *She,* bounded from every other *He* or *She,* a specific point in space and time within the net of the world; nor is he a nature able to be experienced and described, a loose bundle of named qualities. But with no neighbor, and whole in himself, he is *Thou* and fills the heavens. This does not mean that nothing exists except himself. But all else lives in *his* light.
>
> Just as the melody is not made up of notes nor the verse of words nor the statue of lines, but they must be tugged and dragged till their unity has been scattered into these many pieces, so with the man to whom I say *Thou.*[29]

Other conceptions and working relations with media exist that are more productive than the ones we commonly hold. The conception of the relationship between image maker and media that is held by many primal people, for example, will provide much for us to consider. For primal people, there are no things or events in the universe that are merely soulless, insensate, purposeless things. For such societies, the whole universe is alive and purposeful, possessed of inner spirit. Their task is to become aware of the hidden but present life that animates everything and to engage with that "other" so as to honor its essence, respect its distinct inherent legitimacy of being, and appropriate its special powers for one's own use with gratitude. When the things from which power and sustenance are appropriated are cared for, the things themselves yield to the person's requests and permit the usage of their powers. As Buber puts it, when we speak to the "other" as a "Thou" it speaks to us as "Thou." When we address the other as "it," the other responds in kind by speaking to us only of its "itness," and speaking to that in us that is "it." In this way, both we and our perceivable world are diminished.

Taking things from the world for our own devices ought not to be a casual affair. When we appropriate things of the world for ourselves—cut a tree down, kill an animal to feed or clothe ourselves, break and collect stones, plow the earth, divert the river—we are disturbing the universe. Any taking shifts the exquisite balance of the world, a world that is not ours to own, but in which we are a temporary guest. And we must act accordingly. It is wrong to kill, to take things, to bruise things, to deny things their inalienable rights. Especially so when we are rather fragile things ourselves, guests in a home of great beauty, overseen by omniscient and omnipotent deities (or natural forces, if you will) that are not indifferent to our behavior. In the world held by primal people, one engages with the world carefully and with respect, or not at all.

The anthropologist T. C. McLuhan has beautifully conveyed the special affinity that indigenous people have traditionally had with the land.

> The occasion . . . was an Indian council in the Valley of Walla Walla in 1855 . . . to set up three reservations. . . . Young Chief, of the Cayuses, opposed the treaty and grounded his objections on the fact that the Indians had no right to sell the ground which the Great Spirit had given for their support. He gave the following speech before signing away their land.
>
> I wonder if the ground has anything to say? I wonder if the ground is listening to what is said? I wonder if the ground would come alive and what is on it? Though I hear what the ground says. The ground says, It is the Great Spirit that placed me here. The Great Spirit appointed the roots to feed the Indians on. The water says the same thing. The Great Spirit directs me, Feed the Indians well. The grass says the same thing, Feed the Indians well. . . . The Great Spirit, in placing men on the earth, desired them to take good care of the ground and to do each other no harm. . . .[30]

> In the following passage, an old holy Wintu woman speaks sadly about the needless destruction of the land in which she lived—a place where gold mining and particularly hydraulic mining had torn up the earth.
>
> The White people never cared for land or deer or bear. When we Indians kill meat, we eat it all up. When we dig roots we make little holes. When we built houses, we make little holes. When we burn grass for grasshoppers, we don't ruin things. We shake down acorns and pinenuts. We don't chop down the trees. We only use dead wood. But the White people plow up the ground, pull down the trees, kill everything. The tree says, "Don't. I am sore. Don't hurt me." But they chop it down and cut it up. The spirit of the land hates them. They blast out trees and stir it up to its depths. They saw up the trees. That hurts them. The Indians never hurt anything, but the White people destroy all. They blast rocks and scatter them on the ground. The rock says, "Don't. You are hurting me." But the White people pay no attention. When the Indians use rocks, they take little round ones for their cooking. . . . How can the spirit of the earth like the White men? . . . Everywhere the White man has touched it, it is sore.[31]

When a mask maker of a primal society is called upon to provide a mask for a ritual, he proceeds in entirely different ways than we might choose. If we were commissioned to make a mask for a holiday celebration—Halloween, for instance—we would work up some designs, buy some cardboard, fabric, paints, perhaps some wooden dowels and boards, and start cutting, pasting, painting to form the piece in mind. Our work done, we hand over the piece and accept our commission. A straightforward affair.

The primal mask-maker proceeds entirely differently. Masks are not merely decorative things, but a means of increasing one's power to do real and necessary business with the world. Donning a mask is to take on and assume great responsibility for this increase of power. Therefore one does not lightly place a mask over one's face. Nor, since it is ultimately to the gods that requests are made and homage offered, does one engage carelessly in the task of making a mask. The mask-making tradition in Bali, for example, respects this serious intention.

> In Bali there is a deep bond between the maskmaker and the actor who wears the mask in performance. As he sculpts, the woodcarver meditates on the performer who will use the mask as well as on the archetypal character he is trying to represent. He focuses on the needs of that individual actor as well as on the needs of the village in which the performance will take place.
>
> In turn the performer acknowledges his responsibility to the maskmaker's intentions. He does not put on a mask immediately after receiving it. He first enters a period of contemplation during which he studies the character traits expressed in the mask's physical form. During this time the mask is kept in a special place in the actor's family temple. Sometimes he sleeps with it next to his pillow to induce dreams based on its image.[32]

For the primal mask-maker the task does not begin and end with the world of things. Masks and all image making begins, ends, and is entirely to do with evolving from one state of being human to a more elevated state through the agency of ritual and sacred objects. Thus the primal artist begins the creative encounter by working on himself or herself, not by working on wood or paper. Such artists must prepare themselves so as to be acceptable to the powers that be, so that the gods will allow them to be the earthly agents of their powers. Given this extraordinary task, primal artists are required to divest themselves of ordinary living and thinking patterns and to purify, to empty themselves of all that is common so that they may be available to the more subtle and more powerful forces that reside beneath and above ordinary reality. Typically, such artists remove themselves from the company of others and retreat to designated or found places where they can align their consciousness with other dimensions of being. They must attune their perceptual apparatus to those things in the world that are reluctant to reveal themselves to any but the prepared. They must demonstrate that they are worthy to accept the burden of power bestowed upon them by the gods. Worthy, too, to be an agent for their people.

Jamake Highwater has described the primal artist's devoted attentiveness.

I was once given advice by an Indian who was very much worried about my preoccupation with words. "You must learn to look at the world twice," he told me as I sat on the floor of his immaculately swept adobe room. "First you must bring your eyes together in front so you can see each droplet of rain on the grass, so you can see the smoke rising from an anthill in the sunshine. *Nothing* should escape your notice. But you must learn to look again, with your eyes at the very edge of what is visible. Now you must see dimly if you wish to see things that are dim—visions, mist, and cloud-people . . . animals which hurry past you in the dark. You must learn to look at the world twice if you wish to see all that there is to see." [33]

Nothing is incidental to the primal mind; all things play unique and essential roles in keeping the universe spinning just so. Each ceremony and its attendant ritual objects have proscribed taboos and required ingredients. Mask makers may eat only red foods, or no red foods. They may eat only animals they themselves kill, or only those foods that are found ready to eat, such as fallen nuts and berries. They must follow whatever tradition prescribes to purify, tune, and prepare the body to be an acceptable vessel through which the gods may work their will.

And they must likewise prepare the mind. They must carefully cleanse the mind of incidental affairs in order to recognize signs that would pass unnoticed by lesser, clouded minds. So they meditate, dream, chant, wait. As in Zen meditation, the mask maker allows the noise of thought that clouds the mind to become still. And in that stillness comes clarity and heightened awareness.

At some point, cleansed, attuned, and inspired, the primal artist seeks the material that will be appropriated for the task. Here again the process is a slow one. The artist does not simply grab any likely piece of wood or cut down any tree that may capture the fancy. A tree unwilling to yield itself of its powers may be carved into a desired likeness, but such a mask will be an empty affair, contain no power, convey nothing to the gods; worse, it is likely to bring harm to the transgressor who robbed it of its life.

Primal artists intent on important tasks must not upset the balance of the universe without due compensation. They must be patient and alert, they must polish the soul in order to recognize subtle signs that point to chosen places and things. The right tree for the mask is the tree that has been already designated. It is the artist's responsibility to notice the sign and find it. One who is not prepared adequately will not be allowed to find the tree, or may be led to the wrong tree, bringing disaster on the artist and his or her people.

Eventually the mask maker/artist comes upon the tree sought after, in truth the tree that has been provided. Again care and appreciation must

guide the process. Witness this prayer of a Native American as she appropri-
ates the powers of a cedar tree.

> When a woman cuts the roots of a young cedar tree she prays: "Look at me,
> friend! I come to ask for your dress, for you have come to take pity on us; for
> there is nothing for which you can not be used, because it is your way that
> there is nothing for which we cannot use you, for you are really willing to give
> us your dress. I come to beg you for this, long life-maker, for I am going to make
> a basket for lily roots out of you. I pray, friend, not to feel angry with me on
> account of what I am going to do to you, and I beg you, friend, to tell your
> friends about what I ask of you. Take care, friend! Keep sickness away from me,
> so that I may not be killed by sickness or in war, O friend!"[34]

I wonder if we Westerners, given our conception of the world and our
place in it, can imagine the awe with which the indigenous people went
about their daily tasks and walked through this once-unblemished land.

Possessed now of the material and the powers residing within, the artist
moves forward to the next task: to become acquainted with this new element in his or her life, to notice its special features, feel its pulse so that
when the material is eventually touched—cut, painted, or otherwise altered—it is done in a manner that preserves the original life force.

But even this account proceeds too quickly; before the artist takes tool to
material, we ought to consider the special relationship between artists and
their tools. The tools for making sacred objects are not instruments of everyday use; they are employed only for special tasks and are to be used only by
approved handlers. Tools often have long and celebrated histories as they
are passed down along the generations. The tools themselves are semi-
sacred things. In prepared hands they yield the latent images that lie embedded in the substance to be worked. The tools know the way into the heart of
the wood, revealing the spirit residing within the tree, but only for the
adept, only for the initiate who respects the power of the tool. For those
unprepared for their task, the tool uncovers nothing. Worse, it may turn on
its handler, painfully reminding that person of his or her transgressions.

There is, then, a consortium of forces brought to bear on the making of a
mask for primal peoples. There is the mask maker, who tunes his mind and
hand to the task; there is the material from which the mask will be fashioned, which is willing to yield its life force to imbue the mask with its
power; and there are the mask maker's tools, which act as extensions of the
person's own physical prowess. And above these hover the forces of the deities who watch over all, ensuring that all parties are in their right place,
carrying out their assigned roles.

Or take the care with which Japanese tea masters handle the implements used for the tea ceremony. Every item involved in the ceremony is given a full measure of care, from the manipulation of the meticulously carved bamboo tea scoop to the cutting of the charcoal briquettes, to the precise banking of the ashes in the fire box, to the bow securing the tea bag, to the exact, silent placement of the elaborate water ladle on the rim of the water kettle; everything counts for the teamaster, because everything counts in life. The tea ceremony itself, like mask making, is not so much a matter of drinking tea as it is a metaphoric reminder of what life is for and how full of care and reverence it should be lived.

Before guests arrive for a tea ceremony, the host thoroughly cleans both the tearoom and the surrounding garden. Then he lays a fire in the sunken hearth or brazier and puts a kettle on to boil. In the tokonoma, an alcove at one side of the small room, he hangs a scroll and arranges flowers. When the guests arrive, they move silently, in single file, through the garden, rinse their hands and mouths at a stone basin filled with clean water, and crouch to enter through the low doorway of the tearoom. Each guest gazes quietly at the tokonoma for a moment before taking his place in a row facing the hearth where the tea will be prepared.

The host opens the door from the adjoining pantry and greets his guests. He then carries in, group by group, the jar of fresh water; the tea bowl, tea scoop, and tea caddy; and finally the waste-water jar and bamboo ladle [as well as] the kettle, utensils for tending the fire, incense case and burner, and utensils for eating the simple delicacies that are served with the tea or the meal that sometimes precedes it. . . .

After placing all the objects in their proper locations, within easy reach, the host takes his place by the hearth, facing his guests. Using a silk napkin, he wipes the tea scoop and the ladle. After placing the kettle lid on its special stand, he pours a ladleful of water from the kettle into the bowl, washes the bamboo whisk, empties the water into the waste-water jar, and wipes the tea bowl with a clean cloth. Taking up the tea scoop and tea caddy, he puts two scoopfuls of tea in the bowl and replaces the caddy in front of the fresh water jar. He pours a ladleful of hot water into the bowl and whisks the tea into a pale green foam. He presents the bowl to the first guest and bows. While each guest is partaking of his bowl of tea, the host cleans the bowl used by the preceding guest and replenishes the kettle from the fresh-water jar; he returns for the tea caddy and tea bowl, and finally for the fresh-water jar. His bow to the guests from the threshold of the pantry signifies the completion of the ceremony.[35]

In this passage we can feel the uninterrupted grace and flow of the entire choreography of the event as well as the devoted attention paid to every detail. One such detail is the tea scoop, smallest of the items employed in the tea ceremony, a seemingly humble object, a slightly bent strip of bamboo six to eight inches in length.

Tea masters observe a number of important points about a tea scoop, including the bend of the scoop, the treatment of the areas above and below the node,
the node itself, the stem, the curve between the node and the scoop, and the
tip. It is in these points that the particular taste and skill of the maker emerges.
For the tea world, which delights in minute observations, these fine distinctions
are a matter of course. . . .

A tea scoop is a sculptural object, and its appreciation depends upon perception of its sculptural qualities. Looking at a tea scoop is an experience similar to
holding a hand-formed Raku tea bowl in one's hand: not only the skill of the
craftsmanship but also the spirit of the maker himself are to be felt.[36]

One needn't hold to a cosmology animated by the gods and infused with
spirits in order to conceive of and work with media and tools with parallel
respect and care. Even without the belief in a guiding spiritual dimension,
we can still think of media not as mere inanimate things that have to be
manipulated in order to create an expressive image, but as potential sources
of power with which we may ally ourselves. One doesn't have to posit a
spiritual or determinate universe to feel the latent potential residing in different material—the solemn resistance of stone, the veiny aliveness of wood
with its honey warmth.

MEDIA AND THE SACRED

We may look at the issue of a life lived in higher consciousness in still another way. We can say that either we live in a universe in which nothing at
all is sacred or we live in a universe in which everything is sacred. Whatever
the case may be, it is actually unlikely that the universe consists of some
regions and some objects that are sacred and other objects and regions that
are not. To designate some neighborhoods as holy and others as not is a
convenient way to reserve for oneself the privileges which go along with
being on the "right side" of things. No, it is either all one way or the other.
We need, too, to redefine the word *sacred*, so that it is not the exclusive
province of religion or of the supernatural. With equal justification we may
say that *sacred* means whatever is imbued with inherent legitimacy, has an
inextricable history and presence, possesses infinite connectedness with the
rest of the universe, is fundamentally necessary, emerges from unknowable
time and circumstance, extends into an unknowable and infinite future, is
impossible to "own" and forever evolving into unanticipatable outcomes.
Let us call whatever in the universe has these characteristics sacred. And
since all things of the universe do have these qualities, even without making
a case for gods, there is enough evidence that this just might be a sacred
universe. Who knows?

If this is *not* a sacred place, then hell, let 'er rip, let's tear the place apart and gobble up all that we can lay our mitts on because, hey, why not have some fun? Which is pretty much the way we have been behaving lately. If, on the other hand, we choose to believe that the place, all of it, every last crumb, worm, ne'er-do-well, star and moon, all of it is sacred, well, we conduct our lives accordingly. Then everything is met with care, we tread lightly, we move unhesitatingly, we seem heroic but really it is a simple courage born of a feeling of being at home in a rather stupendous universe.

We can consider our media, our tools, as if they were dead things that depend upon us for their worth. We can treat them as expedients, things to be forced to do our will, trashed when they resist. Or we can reach out to them, call to them, come close to them, tame them as they allow their powers to be put to our purposes. And, crazy as it sounds (and crazy as it may be), when we shut the light out in the studio after wrestling with the universe, we might say, to no one or no thing in particular, "Thank you."

Unlike the mask maker whose work is initiated by others and in the service of others, our work mostly derives from inner reasons. If the primal artist finds the appropriate match between what is requested and the materials needed to provide that, how shall we seek appropriate media for our personal intentions when no one compels us and no gods lead us? Faced with the vast array of media at the disposal of artists today—the paints, chalks, fabric, papers, brushes, pens, inks, markers, clays, and so on—and without a purposing, predeterminant world, how shall we choose our allies, how shall we know right from wrong?

There are many ways to respond to this question. The current wave of hedonism favors the method of trying them all. As with food, clothes, and mates, when we get peeved or bored with one, just move on. This time-honored method does work; however, much wreckage is left in its wake. We will explore instead other, less extravagant ways, more in keeping with the philosophy that animates the approach I've taken here.

MEDIA IN THE SERVICE OF EXPRESSION

Before setting out to rummage through the mounds of art supplies stocked in our local art store, suppose we turn inward and tune our own equipment a bit. Before the salesman asks us if it will be acrylic or gouache, or designer colors, or watercolors, or oils or tempera or casein, or inks, suppose we put some questions to ourselves about ourselves.

Before we make strategic decisions as to what material we "need," we will do well to give thought to the match between what we want to say and our choice of an instrument through which to convey that statement. In other words, what alliances can we make with things in the world so as to enhance our power to transform products of the mind to products of the hand? The world at large is a vast jumble of things, the world of art only slightly less vast and jumbled. In this mad zoo, whose inhabitants alternately call to us and hide, we need somehow to find the correct fit between our purposes and the expressive power of each medium. One way to accomplish this is to set up a temporary but useful classification system by slicing the world into halves, each half revealing a telling cross-section.

Thus we can slice the entire universe of art things into a half consisting of things that are two-dimensional, planar, and one made up of all the rest, things that are three-dimensional, spatial. We then have before us two distinctive piles. In the planar pile of art media are paintings, drawings, prints, photographs. In the spatial pile are sculpture, gardens, and architecture. We can also slice the world along the axis of wet and dry. In one pile we have gouache, inks, acrylics, oils, and watercolors, in the other pile we have pencils, charcoals, and pastels. We can slice the world along other critical axes as well, and each time we do so, we reveal another display of the world's dichotomies. Other sample cross-sections are organic/inorganic (e.g., cherrywood/core ten steel) color/tone, hard/soft, permanent/transitive, solitary/collaborative, mobile/stable.

Having cut the world in two, we can now proceed to test the fit between what we want and what the world (media) has to offer. In the following descriptions of several such halvings, the cross sections are examined more closely.

Planar/Spatial

Is what I need to say and the way I need to express it something that requires a surface to support it, hold it in place: a plane, a wall, or a screen? Do I want to plant this in space so that I can approach it from a variety of angles, each one revealing another aspect of what I have to say? Do I want my statement to exist in an invented, controllable space? If so, I have to create my own illusion of space and must do so by fabricating it out of a plane.

Would I rather place my statement in the world of everyday spaces and take my stand and chances there? Here I am at the mercy of people who can approach me from any angle, who can touch me, who can crawl up and under and over me. Do I need air to say my piece fully and well? How much air between me and them do I need, how much above their head, beneath their eyes to tell them what I know?

How close to me do I want them? Too close, and there is the danger of contempt bred from familiarity. Too far, and they are indifferent. Shall I touch the floor? Shall I hover? Shall I assert my position from the center of the room? Shall I stretch toward heaven, creep along the floor?

I want this statement to be clear and emphatic, but I must say it unabrasively or they won't listen. Where shall I stand? What posture shall I assume?

Narrow/Broad Spectrum of Palette

Do I want a severe vocabulary to express myself, eliminating shades of gray, and eschewing the full spectrum? A constrained palette will compel me to make every mark unequivocal, force me to be decisive, take from me any hiding place. Is this what I want? Need I come so bare to the creative encounter?

With black and white I can get directly to the bones of things. I can touch structure, reason, form, and do so raw. With color, I have climate and atmosphere. With color I can tune more exactly feeling, mood, can soak form in color, I can fill space with affective light, leaning on my audience to sway them to see it my way. I can color their experience, nudge them in my direction.

Why not let it all go? Why be so exclusive and hard on myself? Why not let everything in? Life is teeming with outrageous variety, embarrassing behavior; why should I restrain myself? When an infinite circus is whirling around me, why should I be so timid in my choices? Is severe choice a failure of imagination, timidity of spirit, or quite the contrary? On the other hand, is there not something grand in making judicious choices and being satisfied with that? When everyone else is grabbing everything they can get their hands on, isn't it rather brave to be reserved?

There are many other telling sites at which we may make our cross-section cut of the world. With each question, at each cut, we begin to appreciate the enormous power of expression at our disposal inherent in all media. The important feature in choice of media is not what *medium* we use but what *statement* we wish to make. Then we may ask ourselves what substance to choose as our ally in saying what needs saying.

It was suggested at the outset of this chapter that it is useful to shift the association we make with the materials that artists employ from the static inventory of things inferred by the term *art supplies* to the more dynamic and intermediary qualities implied by the term *media.* Exploring the implications of this transposition further, we can say a number of things about how media serve expression.

Media are things that *transform* thought into action. All things when moved from the domain of thought to the physical domain exist in time, place, substance, and movement. *Every* medium therefore consists of these four qualities. The basic character of each medium is determined by the degree to which each quality is *exploited.* It is important to note that every medium has infinite potential in each category—time, place, substance, and movement. And it is *we* who choose to manifest any one or more of its potential qualities and conversely to delimit the active expressive presence of the others.

Thought of in this way, the most humble media exhibit infinite potential. To illustrate this point, let us take the humblest of all art media, the cheap and ubiquitous crayon. Instead of using crayons conventionally to make a picture of a house, a tree, or what have you, we can exploit two rarely used dimensions of crayons: time and space. We can denude the crayons of their wrappers, exposing cylinders of color. Suppose we do this to about one hundred crayons, the cost of about one tube of Winsor & Newton Rose Madder. Let's suspend these miniature cylinders of color from various lengths of thread, tying each end to an overhead grill. We now have color cylinders in space whose intervals, hues, tones, and values we can arrange to fit our mood or theme.

Suppose we now have a small rotating fan to gently blow through and animate the suspended colored cylinders. Now, if we want to create a denser, more complex aesthetic environment, we can put in several light sources, each of a different color. Positioned at various angles, they shine through the oscillating rain of colored cylinders, casting bands of shifting colors on the surrounding walls.

Why not take this exploitation of the humble crayon's potential still further? Suppose we beat a simple rhythm to the movement of the crayons and the shadows and lights they project. If still more drama is needed for our intentions, we can stand between the suspended crayons and the wall upon which the light from the bulbs is falling and move to what we see, what we hear, and what we feel. Voilà—the crayon transformed.

We could take another trite and overused material—feathers, for example—and retrieve their potential as transformative devices. Think of the Native American war bonnets, the feather capes of the Incas, or the masks of the Sepik River New Guineans. In each case the feather, vested with symbolic meaning, is used to transform ordinary space and time and substance, elevating the ordinary to the extraordinary. Viewed in this way, there are no "art supplies" because everything is supply for creative expression. Further, all substances, no matter how slight, even beans, feathers, or crayons, have the same four powers, each with infinite range. Even a feather occupies time and space and is substance and movement. Winsor & Newton paint, Carrera marble, Belgian linen, rosewood, and glass occupy no additional categories.

There are no humble or limited materials. There are only humble, limited uses—and these uses stem from humble, limited thinking.

We do well to appreciate that our reasons for choosing which traits of a medium ought to be exploited should not be merely decorative impulses but the same sorts of reasons that impel us to employ any language, that is, the desire to convey something meaningful in an effective manner. Suspending the crayons, casting light upon them, causing them to be blown around ought to be motivated by this same need. If a crayon used to make colored line demarcations is an articulate way of communicating what needs to be said, do it. If a crayon used as colored form moving in space is a better vehicle for saying what needs to be said, do it.

The powers of every substance stretch in all four directions of time, space, substance, and movement. The question is, how far does our mind stretch? How far are we willing to go in pursuit of finding the means to say what has to be said? How far are we willing to go in the exploration of time, space, substance, and movement in order to say what we must say?

We can take an even closer look at the process of determining the correct fit between what we wish to say and our media. At this close-up level the process is seen as not so much deliberate and rationally systematic as somatic. At this point of contact between ourselves and our media, something actually happens to our physical, our sensual bodies. Instead of willfully choosing our media, we may so place ourselves in relation to them that the media choose us or, more precisely, that they call to us to be chosen.

PAPERS I HAVE KNOWN

On many occasions I have felt the need to work but have been uncertain about the direction that appetite seemed to be taking. I have at such times put aside any sense of urgency I may have had to make a "thing" as an outcome of this creative "itch" and instead put that energy to touching, seeing, smelling the heaps, piles, and stacks of stuff in my studio. I have dozens of kinds of paper in my studio. For me, the marriage between the instrument that yields a mark and the vehicle that receives and retains the mark is critical, often inspirational. There are days when I rummage through my stack of paper with no particular project in mind. I take a sheet out and bring it over to the window, enjoying its flutter as I walk across the studio. Holding it up to the light, I like to scan the sheet for its special patina of irregularities. I like the slightly hilly quality of paper, it offers me something more than a slick, utterly flat surface. No, I shouldn't say "more," I should say "different," for I am often perked up by the creamy, smooth slab of a thick-coated stock.

I like to observe the arabesques paper sheets make when they bend over on themselves. Translucent, these tissue-thin sheets have a way of collapsing down upon themselves that really is piteous. No fiber, no guts, but a wonderful fragility that demands a delicate touch. Very Victorian, with all the swoons and fainting spells one expects (and enjoys). Often I'll hold the paper obliquely to the light and seek its rhythms of impressions (imparted, no doubt, by the paper rollers at the mill as it was squeezed through). In some papers the indentations are deep and wide, creating emphatic pools of shadow and peaks of light. Charcoal rubbed across these peaks yields brilliant spots of inky black, while the valleys remain chaste. The contrast between the crisp blacks and whites immediately excites the surface and causes a stir, the echoes of which are felt all across the sheet.

Other papers, as slick as ice, seem to want something to slide across their backs. Jet black ink seems to be called for from the sidelines here. The ink seems forever alive and wet on these icy lakes. The edges of black cut so finely against the implacable whatevers of the sheet.

Some papers have an open weave, with zillions of tiny fibers making a closely woven felt mat. I love touching this paper. There is so much tactile information here that I close my eyes while passing my hands over its surface. The sensations coming to me through my fingers and palms are all that my brain can handle, it seems; information from my eyes would just overwhelm the circuits. These dense mats turn black charcoal to gray, the fibers contending with the charcoal for the light. Sometimes I try to fight this with many passes of the charcoal over the surface, or by rubbing the particles into the fiber with my palm. But more often I'll work into that surface with some cooler, softer grays. They tend to like each other better, promoting rather than contending with one another's inherent qualities. This marriage leaves a dreamy surface, edges imperceptibly merge, colors sink back into the page, creating an indefinite space within which the image resides. The sheet reflects no highlights, gives off no sheen, and therefore takes in all the light that comes its way, slowly giving back again only what is necessary.

I like tearing paper. I like to hear paper when I tear it, it tells me a lot about what's inside that paper, how it was made, how strongly its fibers were woven, how one side is structurally different from the other, what the inside looks like. Paper for me is not a simple plane. It is no more simple or two-dimensional than a leaf. Both have a top and bottom and middle (I mean in cross section). I learn a lot about my paper by feeling it resist me when I tear it. It tears differently side to side than it does top to bottom. Tearing sounds like a rather ruthless thing to do, and I don't mean it that way . . . but then again, sometimes I do.

And what about the infinite hues, tones, and values that paper comes in! Where to begin with this? Let's just call all these qualities of color *color.*

Color establishes the overall emotional climate within which the creative encounter takes place. It sets the tone, not an exact mood, but a proprietal range. One can, of course, insert any image, declaring any emotional attitude one wishes, into a given context. The effect is similar to that produced by a guest at a formal affair who barges in with a suede jacket, chinos, and topsiders. You can do it, but it will be noticed.

Just as I have discussed paper here, we could also describe how any material may call to us. Each material, like each person in our lives, has its own special interior life. If we can open ourselves to our materials, they will reveal themselves to us. But they will do so only as long as we do not violate them, push them, shove them around. Treating them that way indicates that we no longer are engaged in a respectful partnership. Instead we have become adversaries, and as we strive to master them they resist us, elude our grasp, refuse to yield their natural prowess.

Well, how can we *know* when the paper calls to us? When we feel ourselves quicken somewhere within, we know a connection between us and the other has been made. People, flowers, sunsets, pictures do the same thing. We may not know what we want, but when we see it, we recognize it immediately. Call it sympathetic vibes, harmonic complementarities, love at first sight. Whatever. Something within quickens, the heart, the eyes, the nose, the guts. Wherever, if we allow ourself to be available to it, unhurried and attentive, with no prior agendas, it comes.

There need not be gods calling to us to tell us we are in the right vicinity, that the fit between what we seek and what there is before us is exact. The process can be much more secular than that. Whatever the source, the tingle is still the same and it will happen. What we need to do is to become aware of that tingle and heed it.

6

Commencement

WILL YOU JOIN THE DANCE?

Throughout these pages parallels have been drawn between life and art, and both have been described as embarking upon a journey. I have asserted that there is a similarity between how we create a particular kind of journey through time and space—and thus address life—and how we address the open plane of the canvas. It may also be said that there are two basic stances in regard to life and art: each stance or journey affords different rewards and exacts different costs.

The first stance in response to life may be described as one of acquisitiveness. From this perspective, the world is perceived as something like a giant department store and the aim of the enterprise (life) is to accumulate as many things as we can before the closing buzzer sounds. Success means having acquired a lot of things in our allotted (if unspecified) amount of time. Another wrinkle to this point of view is that not only do we have to get a lot of things but they have to be highly valued things. A hundred boxes of Pampers counts less than a hundred Rolex watches.

People who play this game well know where the "good" stuff is and have a game plan to get there in the shortest time. The successful ones make it out the door loaded with stuff just as the buzzer sounds and, of course, the game—and they—are over. These are clever people, lucky people, in the right place at the right time. They accumulate lots of nice things.

Such people are sometimes artists, but rarely. Seldom are these people visionaries, for they cannot afford to dally along the way, to become caught up in the rapture of vast horizons, of detail and subtlety. They have little time for daydreaming. They rarely venture into dark and uncharted places. They do not stop to gaze into the mirror, inspect carefully what is there and what is not there. They rarely stop to examine the rules of the game, to test the soundness of the goals or the efficacy of their means. They do not fret over tuning their instrument, voicing it just right. More is better, much more is much better. They seldom have time for slow dancing, soft touching. They do not stop in the hurly-burly of the game to look up and wonder at the stars. They do not take long walks and come back with empty pockets. They cling to things. They desire, need, require things, many, many things to slake their insatiable appetites.

In contrast to this type, with its requirement for possessions, the artist, although a maker of things, does not cling to them. For the creative person the thing is only the residue of the past, a record of the journey to date. It is a point of orientation and point of departure. Wonderful as a marker, never a destination.

Rather than the world conceived as a department store and the self as a supershopper, the other stance in response to life is the one that creative people tend to take. This perspective takes life to be not so much a place but an endless dance and the self to be a dancer with an endless stream of partners, bidden and unbidden, who appear, then disappear, only to have the next appear. Each partner asks, Will you dance? With each partner there is different music, and a different setting. Will you dance? Will you dance the same way you did before with your new partner and to new music? Will you sit this one out? Will you seek out your next partner? Will you wait to be asked? Will you request new music? Will you try a new step? Will you? Won't you? Will you join the dance?

What's the point of this game? I don't know. I do know that life is different for those who dance, and for those who do not, for those who only do the two-step, and those who make up their own steps, for those who sit out the fast stuff, and those who squeeze their partners. It's like that for artists as well.

ON RETURNING TO OLD FRIENDS, IN NEW WAYS

The engagement with the creative process is a call to change, to awake and move on. If the engagement has been full, things will not be the same for you as they were. Just as the look and feel of your art will change, just so will you yourself change. The experience of returning to old and dear associates who have not been party to our evolution and most likely have not themselves changed in the meanwhile is a most important and sensitive matter. This final note offers counsel on returning to old friends in new ways.

We conduct our affairs throughout much of our life in a semisomnam-bulant fashion. We go about doing what needs to be done, saying what ought to be said. We derive satisfaction from some portions of our life, other portions leave us flat, empty. Whatever our status, the fit between the world and ourselves is rather exact. We know our world, and we act accordingly.

The world knows us, and reacts to us accordingly. We all play out our roles and expectations in a close choreography of self-fulfilling prophecies. We mostly hate things that we are supposed to hate and love the things we should love. People we would expect to admire us do, people who shouldn't, usually don't. We may not like the drama we are in and then we resist it, but even here we do so in rather predictable ways. Everything fits so nicely together. Cops chase robbers, robbers chase easy marks, lovers chase each other.

The point of this perhaps too lighthearted exegesis is that we are who we are and the world is the way it is because we are who we are. Now, if you no longer are the person you were, you will perceive the world differently, you will behave differently to the world, and the world must behave differently to you as well. There's the rub: it's not so easy for the world to change just like that and just for you. The world, and here I mean the people in the world, resist change, get upset and confused by change even though change they must.

To apply this broader perspective to our case in point: when you change, you will have to alter your relationship with the people dearest to you, and those who love you will have to change their relationship with you. This accommodation is not automatic; it is sometimes difficult, always necessary. It deserves our serious attention. Therefore let us examine the matter further.

If your experiences with the Creative Encounters have been effective, you will return to your loved ones more than likely more exuberant about life. There may be a greater edge to your appetite for expressing and receiving fuller emotions. What will these same folks do, they who have known you and loved you as a dear but more reserved person? How can they know what changes have occurred within you? You look the same from the outside, but unbeknownst to them something essential has been added to your sense of self—and some other things may now be missing.

You are likely to feel somewhat disoriented as you reenter familiar places, which may now feel slightly unfamiliar, perhaps more cramped or unexpectedly delicious. As a consequence your emotional life may be at variance with your outer life. You may feel that your new exuberance is not being reciprocated, that your heightened aesthetic sensibilities are going unrecognized. The honesty and fullness on your part in the conversation is not returned as you would want it. If you have worked in the company of others, the degree of communion you may have experienced with your fellow artists may be difficult to achieve initially with your dearest loved ones. As a result of this dissonance you may naturally feel somewhat alienated, saddened, tired, or confused, as if something important is missing. Every veteran of every campaign—be it a war, a college education, a ritualized coming of age, or a major gain or loss—every veteran returns home a new person to a new house and must find a way to make it home.

The return, as disconcerting as it may be, is also wondrous and good. Old things take on a new sparkle. Things used but unseen now emerge from the background, and dear ones become more complex and multidimensional as we find new ways to appreciate them. The ordinary becomes extraordinary. And it is catching. Others are excited by our enthusiasm and extend their reach to us as we reach further toward them.

How to go about this delicate work of accommodation? *Go slowly.* Realize what is at hand and appreciate the scope of the task for all. Practice patience, work on your humility, remain in contact, don't withdraw from the fray, learn new ways to listen, new ways to understand these dear people who are trying to understand you. Go slowly, but not backward.

Naturally it is far easier to declare these precepts than to execute them; however, you do have important experiences now to draw you onward. The same creative energies you brought to bear upon the resolution of your creative encounters can be employed in dealing with the issue of accommodating the new to the old. For instance, you may start sharing your new self with perhaps just one other person whom you trust. It's important that you be the person you now are, but it is not necessary to expose all of the newness to all of your circle at once. One trusted confidant will do initially. When you feel sufficiently "known" to this person, approach another, then perhaps others. All the while these "first" others will prepare the way for the new you by speaking with still others, creating more opportunities for you to be fully the person you have decided you prefer to be.

Go quietly, slowly, and with love.

There will be times when you may become exasperated with others who seem not to catch on quickly enough to the new you. Help them to discover and enjoy this new you. Invite them to engage with you in some of the Creative Encounters; the Visual Dialogues exercise is a particularly inviting and rewarding one to start with, Seeking Your Natural Mark is another one. Create experiences together to fit your particular circumstances. Be as creative here as you were in the creation of your own evolved self.

There may be times when you find yourself nostalgically remembering the exhilarating times you shared with others on your transformative journey as you drew from within. Don't resist this; use this. Why not visualize these memories? Memories are real, they have power to sustain and uplift. They are not a lesser reality, they are but a different category of reality. Enjoy them, allow them to serve your continuing unfolding.

There may be times when you hanker to be with and talk to your recent companions. Do it! Do stay in contact with those who have lived through special moments with you. They share with you unique memories and experiences. Call them, write them, exchange examples of your work. Once again, make of your life what you will. Create opportunities for communion. Sleep surrounds us. Keep awake.

Notes

1. Highwater, *The Primal Mind,* p. 86.
2. Ibid., p. 87.
3. Ibid., p. 81.
4. Ibid., pp. 84, 85.
5. Zinker, *Creative Process in Gestalt Therapy,* p. 16.
6. May, *The Courage to Create,* p. 89.
7. Ibid., p. 96.
8. Highwater, p. 150.
9. Ibid., p. 148.
10. May, p. 64.
11. Ibid., p. 147.
12. Ibid., pp. 53 and 90.
13. Highwater, p. 65.
14. Buber, *I and Thou,* pp. 7, 8.
15. Metropolitan Museum of Art, *Monet's Years at Giverny: Beyond Impressionism,* p. 165 f.
16. Storr, *Guston,* p. 49 f.
17. Kramer, "A Mandarin Pretending to be a Stumblebum," New York Times October 25, 1970 p. B27.
18. Zinker, p. 8.
19. Ibid., p. 5.
20. Field, *On Not Being Able to Paint,* pp. 119–121.
21. Zinker, p. 9.
22. May, p. 107.
23. Buber, p. 10.
24. Ibid., p. 11.
25. Ibid.
26. May, pp. 91–92.
27. Ibid., p. 78.
28. Ibid., p. 97.
29. Buber, pp. 8, 9.
30. McLuhan, *Touch the Earth,* p. 8.
31. Ibid., p. 15.
32. Jenkins, "Two Way Mirrors," pp. 18–19.
33. Highwater, p. 75.
34. McLuhan, p. 40.
35. Fujioka, *Tea Ceremony Utensils,* p. 11.
36. Ibid., pp. 56–58.

References

Buber, Martin. *I and Thou.* Translated by Ronald Gregor Smith. 2d ed. New York: Charles Scribner's Sons, 1958.

Field, Joanna [Marion Blackett Milner]. *On Not Being Able to Paint.* Los Angeles: J. P. Tarcher, 1957.

Fujioka, Ryōichi, et al. *Tea Ceremony Utensils.* Translated and adapted by Louise Allison Cort. New York: Weatherhill, 1973.

Highwater, Jamake. *The Primal Mind: Vision and Reality in Indian America.* New York: New American Library, 1982.

Jenkins, Roy. "Two Way Mirrors: Eastern and Western Versions of Mask." *Parabola* 6, no. 3 (August 1981): 17–21.

Kramer, Hilton. "A Mandarin Pretending to be a Stumblebum" *New York Times,* October 25, 1970 p. B27.

May, Rollo. *The Courage to Create.* New York: Bantam Books, 1976.

McLuhan, T. C., comp. *Touch the Earth: A Self-Portrait of Indian Existence.* New York: Pocket Books, 1972.

Metropolitan Museum of Art *Monet's Years at Giverny: Beyond Impressionism.* New York: Harry N. Abrams, Inc. Publishers, 1978.

Storr, Robert. *Guston.* New York: Abbeville Press, 1986.

Zinker, Joseph. *Creative Process in Gestalt Therapy.* New York: Vintage Books, 1978.